THE DECLINE OF THE AMERICAN EXPERIMENT:

Politics, Economics and Opportunities for a Healthier Democracy

I0415447

GREGORY K. PETTY

ISBN13: 978-1-0922-8717-3
ISBN10: 1-0922-8717-5

Email: gregstours14@gmail.com
Facebook: facebook.com/GregKPetty

Credits:
Editors: Barbara Petty, Cindy Brookshire
Design/Layout: Victor Rook

This book is dedicated to my wife Barbara who has spent many years being an attentive and excellent listener. She was also a sometime critic of my political views but has always been supportive of my passion for good governance.

CONTENTS

PREFACE

The genesis of this book was a series of articles, *Revitalizing Our Democracy,* I wrote in previous years as publisher of *Boom! Magazine.* They concerned the state of our union and steps we could take to enhance our modern democracy.

Chief among our challenges are the threats posed to our nation and the world by climate change. An old issue is still relevant and that is the unprecedented levels of our national debt. Everything else discussed here falls by the wayside if we do not seriously address both of them. Thus, these are the first two issues discussed. Other issues of importance, as addressed in chapter three *(Dysfunction),* have presented themselves. I have updated and edited the original articles and included new material **(in bold type)** as called for by the unprecedented times we now find ourselves. There will be some redundancy between the chapters *Dysfunction* and *Saving American Democracy* due to the fact that some of those issues, five years apart, are still relevant.

I have included some solutions to the various issues addressed herein and it is my hope that this book not only stimulates discussion and additional solutions to the blockades, but action by concerned citizens. Americans need to act together to remove the obstacles that have been placed in front of our republican institutions.

"Prudence, indeed, will dictate that Governments long established should not be changed for light and transient Causes; and accordingly all Experience hath shown, that Mankind are more disposed to suffer, while Evils are sufferable, than to right themselves by abolishing the Forms to which they are accustomed. But when a long Train of Abuses and Usurpations, pursuing invariably the same Object, evinces a design to reduce them under absolute Despotism, it is their Right, it is their Duty, to throw off such Government, and to provide new Guards for their future Security." -The Declaration of Independence

OUR GRAVEST CHALLENGE: CLIMATE CHANGE

Written February 2019

"When all the trees have been cut down, when all the animals have been hunted, when all the waters are polluted, when all the air is unsafe to breathe, only then will you discover you cannot eat money." -Cree Prophecy

Image by WikiImages from Pixabay

FEMA flood maps are now obsolete. Hurricane Harvey in 2017, which struck the Houston-

Beaumont area, was the third 500 year flood (1 percent chance of occurring in any year)—in fact it was a 1 in 1000 year event. At least 30 inches of rain fell over an area the size of Maryland. Hurricane Florence was the same for the states of North and South Carolina. Rainfall records were broken and meteorologist's claimed they had never seen or discovered anything in the historical records to compare either hurricane to. Now emergency officials along the Eastern Seaboard are revising their models to also account for river flooding instead of just wind and tidal surges near the coast.

Since the early 90s countries across the globe, and most notably the United States, have ignored, challenged or outright denied the facts about climate change that scientists have been alerting us to. The loss of years of potential action that we may indeed live to regret.

Climate Facts as Reported by the UN Intergovernmental Panel on Climate Change

- Each year more than 40 billion tons of carbon dioxide are emitted into the atmosphere. China at 10.15 B and the U.S. at 5.31 B are the two leading emitters followed by Land Use Change (cutting down forests) 4.5 B and India at 2.3 B.
- We are at a tipping point to keep carbon emissions from causing more than a 2.7 Fahr-

enheit percent increase in global temperatures and subsequent worldwide destruction of vital habitats.

- Scientists are alarmed at the rapid increase and magnitude of Arctic, Antarctic and Greenland ice sheet melting far surpassing their previous model predictions. The entire global ecosystem from ocean circulation, weather patterns and the way the atmosphere warms are all controlled by what happens in these regions.

From Center for Biological Diversity

- We are in the midst of the world's sixth extinction event. The worst loss of plant and animal species loss since the dinosaurs 65 million years ago. According to the Center, "[Specie extinction]…a natural background rate of about one to five species per year. Scientists estimate that we are now losing species at 1,000 to 10,000 times the background rate, with literally dozens going extinct every day."

I could go on and on with a litany of the deleterious effects we human beings are having on this precious, rare speck of water and rock floating through a harsh and unforgiving universe. We have no other viable planet home that we can realistically travel to or survive on. The facts are all available—the climate deniers just have to pull their heads out of the sand and have the guts to realize these facts, have a change of heart and join the movements for action. As a grandfather, no less than the survival of our children and grandchildren depends on those who hold political and economic power on the earth. Through inaction at best, and naked greed at worst, after years of evidence, they have now left us and all the other species on this magnificent planet, little time to turn back from catastrophic change.

I hold the most disappointment and scorn for the Trump Administration. Not only has it continued this deadly folly by denying reality, it has scaled back Obama's auto emission standards (largest carbon emitting pollutant) and pulled the U.S. out of the Paris Accords. So let's cut to the chase, the UN report tells all of the citizens of the world, and our leaders, that we need to be getting to net zero carbon emissions within the next 10-11 years to halt the worst environmental effects. We have no time to lose. We are at Malcolm Gladwell's *Tipping Point.*

DEBT: AMERICA'S ECONOMIC DEFICITS

Written May 2009 (Updates in Bold)

America is in deep economic trouble...I know this is not a news flash. But it is not the economic crisis that has occupied our government since 2008, the bursting of the housing bubble and the collapse of our financial institutions requiring government bailout to the tune of trillions of dollars. The current crisis is but a symptom of the deeper economic conditions and fiscal direction that we have allowed our political and business leaders to take us. But it is also the story of what financial condition we as individuals have allowed our economy and personal finances to become mired in. Think quicksand. Here are a few other descriptions of our collective economic condition: delusional spending, fiscally bankrupt, morally indefensible debt inheritance.

With few exceptions the media, economists, politicians and business people are not telling Americans the unvarnished (and extremely scary) truth of our long-term financial condition. It is akin to being a patient in the emergency room after a horrendous car wreck and no one wants to tell the family what condition you are in because the news is so bad. This article is intended to spell out some of the brutal facts Americans need to recognize, reflect on, and then take collective action. No one is going to come to America's rescue for very much longer. There are many things at stake starting with our retirement, the future of our children and our grandchildren and ultimately the stability of the global economy. The U.S. dollar is the world's reserve currency but it may not continue to be so if we do not get our house in order.

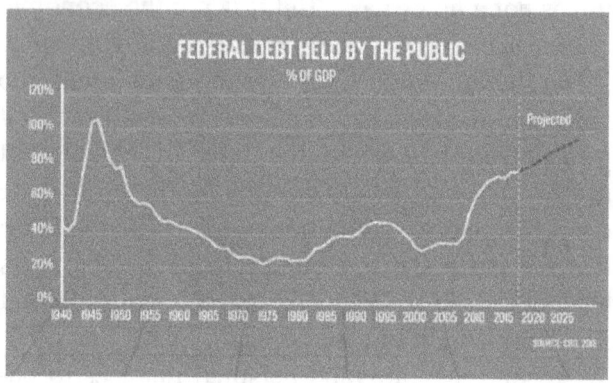

The Current Situation

Unfortunately the current economic situation **(2008 Financial Crisis)** calls for our newly elected government to be the spender of last resort to help restore our economic activity. It has added huge amounts of debt to an already substantial national deficit but is a necessary evil. We cannot allow the crisis to cascade into a true depression.

Here's the trick though. Congress and the Obama administration have to stop this stimulative spending as soon as we are certain the economy has righted itself. Americans need to monitor the following three actions over the course of the next few years:

1. How our money is being spent and returned to us.
2. Demand that a new financial regulatory system be installed that directly addresses the myriad causes that brought us here. Consider reinstating Glass-Steagall [1999 Gramm Leach Bliley repeal of the 1933 regulation separating banking, insurance, securities investment firms] in a modern form and eliminate the concept of banks which are "too big to fail."
3. Congress, with bi-partisan support, must reinstate "pay-go" spending rules that previously stopped annual budget deficits and that Congress conveniently allowed to expire in 2002. As soon as the economy recovers, every expenditure must be paid for or another expenditure dropped.

If we do not stop printing and distributing money through the Federal Reserve, and we allow annual budget deficits to continue, we will add another crisis, the spectre of inflation, to our table already overflowing with crises.

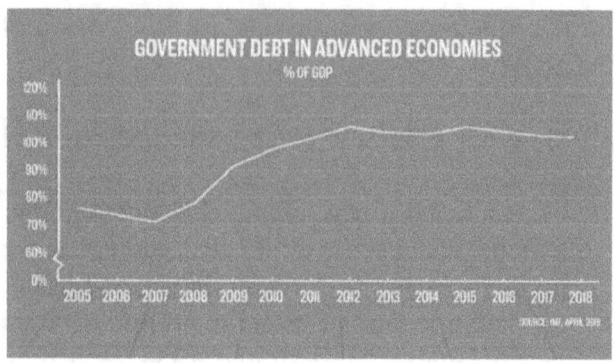

One Deficit, Two Deficits, Three Deficits, Four

The painful truth is that our nation faces multiple deficits that are only going to worsen with time. Strangely enough the time to act is now while we are in a crisis. Action now is important for a whole variety of reasons not the least of which is the moral descriptor I mentioned in the opening paragraph. It is morally indefensible for the current generations to refuse to live within our means, pile up national debt and leave the bill to our children, grandchildren and their children. As former Treasury Secretary Robert Rubin put it simply, "Economics is not that complicated…There is no free lunch."

Number One: Budget Deficits

Here are the facts. They are not Democratic facts or Republican facts but the cold hard truth. Our political leadership, Congress and Executive, have only passed five budgets that resulted in surpluses in 40 years.

Our cumulative national debt now exceeds ten trillion dollars and has been significantly escalated by the current crisis. **2018 Debt—$21.4 trillion**

If we do not reform health care, and its attendant ever-increasing costs, (1) and adjust the funding for the programs of Medicare, Medicaid and Social Security [remove cap on salary tax]these programs will take up the entire federal budget. To quote former Comptroller of the U.S. David Walker, "By the time today's college graduates are ready to retire forty years from now, the only things our government will be able to pay for are the interest on the federal debt and some of the Social Security, Medicare and Medicaid benefits. All other parts of the federal government will be closed and out of business."

Our budget deficits are financed by other nations the largest of whom is China. ($1.3 trillion) This restricts our economic and political alternatives at home and abroad.

Washington is broken. After our immediate crisis (**2008 financial crisis**) is over we need to decide what we want our government to do and then have the fiscal discipline to enforce the mandate to pay down our debt. The pressure has to come from the American people. No politician will do it on their own and not without being pushed. We need a political paradigm shift…and soon.

Number Two: Trade Deficits

This is a simple one to explain but the problem is difficult to reverse. Americans are importing and paying for more than we produce, export and get paid for. In short, we have stopped producing commodities and instead are consuming them.

> Between 2001 and 2007 the U.S. lost 2.3 million jobs, including 1.5 million manufacturing jobs. (2)

The top two U.S. trade deficits from 2007 – China—$262 billion, Oil Exporters – 117 billion. (3) **2017—China $375.0 billion**

We must reduce our consumption and increase our production of commodities (this means manufacturing) the world desires. America still needs to make products and we still can make the best products in the world. We have high productivity and educated workers. To quote I.O.U.S.A: One Nation, Under Stress, In Debt, "Last year, the U.S. borrowed 65% of all the money that was borrowed in the world – 10 times as much as the next biggest borrower."

Number Three: Savings Deficits

I'll give it to you short and straight. The personal savings rate in America in 2007 was 1% and crossed over into a **negative figure** in 2008. We are spending more than we earn. To give you some comparisons, at the end of the 1970s our savings rate was approximately 13 percent. This figure is vital to our economy because it represents real wealth creation from which an economy can prosper and grow. Currently our savings rate accounts for only two percent of our economy, in China it accounts for 40 percent.

After years of barrage by Madison Avenue to go out and consume, it appears we really took it to heart. Some people used their homes as if they were ATM's. Now we must stop. We simply must save for our future. Think back to how your parents behaved...they were raised in the Great Depression and had much better financial discipline. If we don't have the cash, we don't buy it. This is the personal responsibility that we have to start exhibiting.

Number Four: Action Deficit

Take action. On a personal level assess your situation and make any changes you feel are warranted. Pay down debt and save more? Put more funds away for retirement or make new investments? Discuss sound budget, savings, spending and credit with your children.

Collectively we need to ask our Washington officials what their proposals are to stop and reverse these deficits when our economy rebounds. Tell them you are behind them for tough decisions and that spending cuts will be needed. Now is the time for Congress to assess all programs and their effectiveness... if it is not working then stop the funding. If its effectiveness has not been studied then study it. Inquiring minds want to know right now.

And here is the other hard truth we must face. No politician wants to tell you what they know to be true. They are afraid they won't get reelected. Tell them you will support them if they vote to raise taxes... but only if they also vote to reinstate pay-go.

We also have to raise taxes because the deficit we have created for ourselves is so massive that the economy cannot grow its way out. There is no supply-side solution.

Ask them to explain their plan for a reformed, fair and simplified tax code. The current tax code is over 70,000 pages long! But remember, there is no free lunch... Our new mantra is "cut spending, raise taxes." Never again should Americans let both sides of the economic equation be so totally out of balance.

As the words of the Eric Clapton song go,

Tell the truth, tell me who's been fooling who?

(1) Peter Orzag, OMB, PBS Frontline "Ten Trillion and Counting"
(2) The Economic Policy Institute
(3) I.O.U.S.A. One Nation. Under Stress. In Debt. By Addison Wiggin, Kate Incontrera, ISBN# 978-0-470-22277-5 (Book

and DVD Nominated for the 2008 Sundance Grand Jury Prize)

November 2018 Update

During this election season it has been repeatedly pointed out by various media outlets that there are all kinds of issues being discussed before the mid-terms but why isn't our strong economy one of them? Instead we have fear mongering of migrant caravans and who did what on healthcare.

Now is precisely the time that we need to take advantage of our strong economy to reduce our national debt. We need to do it while the economy is robust and before another crisis robs us of the ability to control spending and reduce debt. Arthur Laffler is still out there trumpeting his failed economic supply-side policy (trickle down) and apparently some policymakers still give it credence even though there is no empirical evidence to support it.(See Appendix)

Due to the Trump-GOP tax bill passed in 2017 the 2018 budget deficit will exceed $770 billion. Surprise! The CBO states this has caused flat revenues while Congress increased defense spending by $65 billion and $62 billion increased interest on the debt. The trickle down part of supply-side is not happening and has not ever occurred. Corporations enact stock buybacks and the top-percenters and investors put the tax break money in the bank. Where did all the Republicans go who were concerned about their long professed efforts to reduce deficit spending and the federal debt?

Gross federal debt is now an astounding $21.4 trillion, 107.70 percent of GDP. Perhaps a more relevant and revealing number is the debt totals approximately $40,000 for every man, woman and child in these United States. We need to put the debt clock back up in Times Square so the media can show it regularly. Then we need to consistently ask our representatives in Congress "What have you done to reduce the deficit and the federal debt?" Pressure is the only thing that works.

Why does anyone care? It is not a sexy issue and many Americans do not feel comfortable talking about or have been educated about economics. But our debt is central to the health of our society and ability to act. Consider what we lose when the debt overwhelms our economy and our ability to repay it:

- Loss of political and economic influence and flexibility.
- Ability of our children and grandchildren to repay the debt and live in a vibrant, healthy economy.
- Ability to maintain the vital social programs that care for our youngest, neediest and oldest citizens which form the bulwark of a just society.
- Ability to maintain a strong national defense capability.

DYSFUNCTION

Written February 2019

As I pondered editing and updating aforementioned collection of articles, a recurring image came to my mind. That image was the Founding Fathers flipping over in their graves. The Republic they argued over, discussed ad infinitum and finally produced through compromise at the Constitutional Convention in 1787 now bears no resemblance to what they envisioned – a republic with structural checks and balances. Initially, executive and legislative branches populated by enlightened citizen servants who were to hold office for a time then return to their individual pursuits. Judges at the federal level were to serve lifetime appointments in order to remove them from political pressure and reprisal.

James Madison and others did not envision a true democracy even for the limited population that was allowed to vote at the time. They did not trust the majority of citizens (The Mob) to make sensible decisions affecting all of the country. The method of removal was allowing the people to vote for an elected representative in Madison's words "whose wisdom may best discern the true interest of their country." An aristocratic reasonable majority (Senate) would act to "cool" the actions proposed by the people's elected representatives in the House. Senators at the time were then chosen by state legislators rather than direct vote. We have long since removed that cooling effect. Likewise, the chief executive was to be chosen by electors (propertied white men) rather than direct vote to ensure only men of the highest character and judgement were selected.

James and Dolly Madison – Image from Dennis Larsen from Pixabay

The first crack in the intended republican government came about with the election of Andrew Jackson in 1828. The westward expansion of the country had brought Madison's feared "Mob" into the political sphere and put Jackson over the top. Madison would have said the Electors failed to exercise their intended role. Political elites of the time were wary of Jackson's populism and considered him a ruffian. Their fears were not assuaged when his supporters ransacked the White House after the inauguration. In recent times the entire process of selecting a president has been increasingly democratized.

The Democrats increased the number of primary elections involved when JFK was running for office and they have grown in number ever since. The days of the backroom convention deals for selection of the nominee by the party powers that be are now long gone. Democracy, like the horse, has been let out of the barn and there is no turning back.

Ironically, we witnessed two different sides of nominee selection democracy in turmoil during the 2016 election.

Democratic progressives felt the party had too much control through the super-delegate process with the result being the nomination of an experienced but unpopular candidate with many vulnerabilities. The GOP had the opposite problem, a candidate with populist appeal who was truly unprepared or qualified to be the nominee. The overly democratized process inhibited the GOP from controlling their own candidate selection!

The Supreme Court (SCOTUS) does not escape scrutiny in the decline of our republic. In perhaps what may be its worst decision since Bush v Gore, 2000, Citizen United v FEC, 2010, held that political donations were free speech protected by the First Amendment. A corporation or Political Action Committee (PAC) large donation is the same as my free speech? The floodgates for unlimited political donations, without accountability, were thrown wide open. This is the exact opposite of what our political system needs to maintain civility and the dissemination of factual information to assist voters.

If that was not bad enough, as Lawrence Lessig's book *The USA is Lesterland* **(Chapter 5)** reminds us, Representatives spend most of their time in Washington D.C. raising money from donors or spending time with lobbyists instead of dealing with constituents or listening to debate on the floor. Donor concerns dominate while the needs of the people are neglected. Yascha Moun's March 2018 article *America is Not a Democracy* in Atlantic relates " Steve Israel, a Democratic Congressman from Long Island, was a consummate moneyman. Over the course of his 16 years on Capitol Hill, he arranged 1,600 fund raisers for himself, averaging one every four days. Israel cited fund-raising as one of the main reasons he decided to retire from Congress, in 2016: "I don't think I can spend another day in a call room making another call begging for money... I always knew the system was dysfunctional. Now it is beyond broken."

This is readily evident when we see the failure of our elected officials to truly seek solutions and produce legislation on a host of citizen concerns. Congress will act to protect the economic elites (enact President Trump's 2018 tax bill) and narrow interest groups (Drug Companies, gut the Affordable Care Act) but take no action on the actual concerns of the majority of citizens. Every poll shows the majority of Americans want action on: the Dream Act confirmed, drug prices, long overdue immigration reform, sensible gun reform measures to mitigate violence, living wages and the reduction of income inequality, legalized medical marijuana, protections in law for workers and the right to organize.

Our Founders created three branches of government with the intention that they fulfill their role as checks on the other branches. They also envisioned a strong executive who would be checked by Congress and the Supreme Court. That is not the reality we live with today. For decades now Congress has failed in its duty to place checks on the presidency. We now have an executive with almost unlimited power to act without the approval of the legislative branch. The health of our republic depends on changing this situation. America is witnessing a continual presidential campaign road show instead of the tug and pull between two branches of government in search of solutions to our pressing issues. As John Dickerson notes in his May 2018 Atlantic article *How the Presidency Became Impossible,* "The present system elevates the crowd-pleasing qualifications above all others, and sets expectations for what a president can do well beyond what is actually possible in office...As campaigning has become more about performance, the skills required to be president have become more defined by talent on the stump, an almost perfect reversal of what the Founders intended." President as TV celebrity.

Trump's talent as a showman has created the false impression that he is a problem-solver and businessman who can negotiate anything. Instead Donald Trump has become a national nightmare.

- He has refused to divest himself from his businesses (violation of Emoluments clause),
- His campaign is under investigation for possible collusion with a foreign power,
- Shredded normal political and civil discourse,
- Removed the country from the Paris Accord thus denying climate change,
- Damaged our international alliances and standing,
- Initiated unwise trade wars,
- Denounced and mischaracterized Muslims and Hispanics,
- Stands personally accused of sexual indiscretions,
- Threatened the press and incited followers to harass them,
- Denigrated various members of his own Cabinet who stood up to him, as well as Congress, judiciary and the media.
- At the time of this writing the *Washington Post's* truth tracking unit informs us that Trump has uttered in excess of 7,500 lies or misleading statements!

All of this false rhetoric compounded by social media and internet sites have exponentially increased the ability to disseminate information that has no relation to the truth. These means of immediate political gratification (Facebook, Twitter, podcasts) have served to polarize our society to an extent perhaps unseen since the Civil War.

The current GOP leadership has created a situation where no member dares to step out of the party "box" in opposition to the president. To date we have witnessed only two strong moral objections to the many outrageous actions and claims by Donald Trump. Those came from Sen. Jeff Flake and Sen. Bob Corker who both had already announced their intention to retire. At this point we are not witnessing *"Profiles in Courage"* come from this GOP controlled Congress.

Members from both sides of the aisle are waiting for Special Counsel Robert Mueller's report and the several other legal actions against Trump to obtain a full picture of possible charges that could be included in the articles of impeachment.

Regardless, what we are witnessing is no less than the unraveling of the norms of political and social behavior that enabled America to become the leader of the free world.

ALEC AND NORTH CAROLINA

Written February 2019

"It is by the goodness of God that in our country we have those three unspeakably precious things: freedom of speech, freedom of conscience, and the prudence never to practice either of them. - Mark Twain *Following the Equator*

The American Legislative Executive Council (ALEC) is a secretive nonprofit organization that theoretically exists to bring together lawmakers, lobbyists and corporate entities to exchange ideas and produce what they consider "model" legislation. Its meetings and working groups are closed to the media and only until recently those attending the meetings were kept secret. What has emerged, however, are a host of legislative bills on controversial social and economic issues that have been adopted in many states word-for-word.

North Carolina, West Virginia, Oklahoma, Mississippi, Arizona, Kansas, Montana and 34 states in all adopted ALEC model laws, 90 percent of which were proposed by Republicans. Here are a few examples of model acts introduced in various states:

Climate Change – Interstate Research Commission on Climate Change Act – negates the benefit of reducing carbon emissions, provide a state cover for withdrawing from regional climate initiatives

Nondisclosure of "secret" fluids used in fracking with the Disclosure of Hydraulic Fracturing Composition Act

Castle Doctrine – Stand Your Ground law – use of deadly force if under reasonable fear of bodily harm.

Firearms – prevents local jurisdictions from enacting their own gun restrictions, preempt local jurisdictions from filing civil actions against firearms, ammunition manufacturers, dealers, etc.

No Sanctuary Cities for Illegal Immigrants Act – local governments must enforce federal immigration law, criminalizes employment of illegal immigrants and having an illegal immigrant in the car.

Product Liability Act – North Carolina adopted a statute that increases protections for corporations in product liability suits.

ALEC activities are important for citizens across the country to understand.

While I write firsthand about North Carolina below, all state legislatures are being impacted by egregious legislation enacted for special interests without regard for the majority.

Since 2010 North Carolina has experienced some of the most harmful politically one-sided legislative actions in the nation. Extreme gerrymandering by the super-majority Republican legislature in 2010 has taken a state with a 52 percent to 48 percent Democratic voting edge from a 7-6 Democratic Congressional delegation to the current 10 to 3 Republican delegation. This extreme disenfranchisement has been declared unconstitutional by the US Supreme Court. Because of this legislature's delaying actions—and slow moving courts—the state still has experienced skewed election results in 2018.

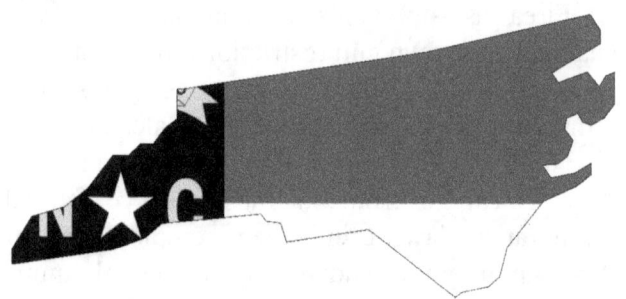

The list of radical actions by the GOP majority legislature in North Carolina include:

- Voter suppression with a Voter ID law declared unconstitutional, changing polling places, shortened early voting dates and reduced voting sites;
- Governor denied expansion of Medicare under the Affordable Care Act to give health care coverage to approximately 500,000 NC residents. 90 percent of cost would have been paid by the federal government. This literally caused suffering and premature deaths due to lack of care and devastated rural hospitals as well as the loss of billions of dollars from our economy. Cutting off your own nose to spite your face!
- Enacted the largest cut to unemployment benefits in history thus becoming the state

that offers the smallest percentage of unemployment assistance;

- The first state to end its Earned Income Tax Credit (EITC), a direct blow to working families;
- Removed over 100,000 qualified people from food stamps which cost the state nothing – entirely paid by the federal government;
- 2012 Amendment to ban gay marriage, passed by voters but declared unconstitutional in federal court;
- Enacted HB2 (The Bathroom Bill) which was a national embarrassment and caused the state to lose millions in revenue when corporations, the NCAA and entertainment acts among others boycotted the state;
- Misled citizens in voting to approve income and tax "reforms" that gave tax cuts to the top five percent and raised taxes on the bottom 40 percent;
- Mass arrests of those opposing these actions at the legislature building and barring citizens from the people's house;
- Made judicial elections partisan, changed the appeals process to limit the state Supreme Court's authority;
- Attempted to overhaul county election boards, change Wake County local commissioner and school board districts;
- Interfered with the power of the Governor to make appointments to boards, reduced the number of state employees who serve at the pleasure of the Governor from 1,500 to 500;

- Made all Cabinet appointments by the Governor subject to Senate approval;
- Removed ability of Governor to appoint any members of the Board of Trustees to administer campuses in the UNC system.

Amendments to the state constitution are rare as they rightfully should be. This legislature has proposed five harmful amendments, and one unnecessary amendment, to the state constitution for the 2018 election. Amendment language has been called by all living past Governors, opposition legislators, the Governor and members of the press, misleading or outright deceptive. Legislative effort has been made to take the writing of the amendment language on the ballot away from the state's Constitutional Amendments Publication Commission as is prescribed.

- Create a voter ID requirement for in-person voting. Voter ID has already been ruled unconstitutional. **This amendment passed 11/6/18.**
- Make 7 percent the maximum possible state income tax. This will unnecessarily limit the ability of the state to deal with unusual financial circumstances. **This amendment passed 11/6/18.**
- Give legislators a major role in choosing and filling judicial vacancies and limiting the Governor's power. **Failed**
- Protect hunting and fishing – Not necessary, it does not need protection. This is simply a

get out the GOP vote measure. **This amendment passed 11/6/18.**

- Change the State Board of Ethics and Elections Enforcement from nine members to eight thereby eliminating the unaffiliated member and making the matters brought before it potentially unresolvable. **Failed**
- Strengthen protections for victims of crimes. Victims already have constitutional rights. What is lacking is the funding for the Victim's Rights offices already in place in local jurisdictions. **This amendment passed 11/6/18.**

The list goes on. As Slate.com noted in December 2016, "What's Happening in North Carolina is not politics as usual. It is an extraordinarily disturbing legislative coup, a flagrant effort to maintain one-party rule by rejecting democratic norms and revoking the will of the voters. It is the kind of thing we might expect to see in Venezuela, not a U.S. state. It should terrify every American citizen who believes in the rule of law. This is so much more than a partisan power grab. This is an attack on democracy itself."

Gene Nichol, UNC law professor, in a May 25, 2018 News & Observer op-ed article opined, "What our General Assembly actually has done, for over a half decade now, is take food, medicine, health (and dental) care, school books, teaching assistants, safe and affordable child care and scarce supporting dollars from poor children in order to give, and then repeatedly expand, massive tax cuts to millionaires and billionaires."

Since 2010, North Carolina has been a one-party state. Under Trump, and the recent GOP Congressional majority, we have seen the emergence of autocracy and Cabinet appointments to clearly unqualified individuals. (Betsy DeVos, Wilbur Ross, Rick Perry, Scott Pruitt) We have watched a televised Cabinet meeting where every member around the table sycophantically praised Trump and reiterated how much they appreciated serving him. We have never experienced anything like it. To quote Hannah Arendt writing in the 1940s about one-party states and the elimination of meritocracy "[one-party states] invariably replaces all first-rate talents, regardless of their sympathies, with those crackpots and fools whose lack of intelligence and creativity is still the best guarantee of their loyalty."

SAVING AMERICAN DEMOCRACY

Written May 2013 (Updates in Bold)

During conversations with friends, family and acquaintances over the last couple of years, the topic returned many times to the subject of what we can do to "save" our democracy. No one seems to be pleased with the direction of our body politic whether you are talking about state or national affairs. Cynicism, during my lifetime, appears to be at its zenith.

Polls show Congressional popularity recently hit an all-time low of 14 percent. **(19 percent September 2018)** As Ezra Klein of the *Washington Post* noted, that ranking "is below lice, colonoscopies and Nickleback." Republicans and Democrats do not mingle with each other, in any way shape or form, in order to try to find common ground and produce results for the purpose they were elected – to accomplish the work of the People. The Senate Republicans have invoked the filibuster (cloture) 60 times in the 2009-2010 session, almost double the other highest point by the Democrats at 38 in 2002-2003. To put this in perspective, cloture was invoked four times in 1965-66 during the Vietnam War – it is not in the Constitution and is not required. It is simply a Senate rule designed to ensure the minority a voice in what the Senate is supposed to be – a more deliberative body.

In April 2017 Republicans invoked the nuclear option requiring only 51 votes to approve a Supreme Court nominee instead of the historical 60. It was used to affirm Neil Gorsuch's nomination to the court. This came after the refusal for over 300 days to bring President Obama's highly qualified nominee Merrick Garland to a vote. This is unprecedented in American history – refusing a president's pick for the court.

We recently watched the process unfold for the nomination of Brett Kavanaugh. Kavanaugh was rushed through before the October SCOTUS session and the November 2018 election in the face of allegations of sexual misconduct and heavy drinking. It then became the most politicized he said/she said testimony this nation has ever witnessed eclipsing even the Thomas/Hill hearing. Before this time we have never seen a nominee needing confirmation shout back at Senators, question and defy them.

No less than the American Bar Association on 9/27/2018 requested by letter that the vote be delayed until an investigation by the FBI is reported to the committee. After an uproar from Judiciary Committee members, Republican and Democrats and the public, Donald Trump then ordered a limited FBI probe. Trump then mislead the American people by stating that the FBI was free to investigate any and all matters.

The rushed and circumscribed FBI report, completed in four days, became immediately suspect for all the people who were NOT interviewed. The report is 46 pages and only one copy was produced. The entire Senate then had one day in a secure location to review this single report before a confirmation vote. The public was not given the report to make their own judgement. Kavanaugh was approved by the Senate with the narrowest of margins.

The vote and confirmation appears to be more important than the character of a man who could serve for life on the nation's highest court and shift the balance of future decisions.

The process is broken, the Senate is broken and extreme polarization is the rule of the day.

Neither the Tea Party or Occupy movements, the far right and the far left, feel that they are represented in Washington D.C. or that proposed laws are addressing the vital issues of the day in effective ways. Those who are in the middle, the great majority, are perhaps even more distressed because neither one of these movements represent the common sense solutions that have the ghost of a chance of becoming law and provide the assurance that compromise is about to break out anytime soon.

In addition to all of the functional pieces of our democracy that seem to have become dysfunctional, we are experiencing economic challenges that we have not faced since the turn of the century and then again in the Depression. I am talking about inequality in our society, the shrinking of the middle class, the loss of jobs and the working man's voice in labor/management relations. As I noted in my article *Goodbye Yellow Brick Road, December 2010,* income distribution between the wealthiest and the least among us is the highest at any time since the time of the Gilded Age of the 1890s. You know the age of the Robber Barons. Back then Americans had Teddy Roosevelt to break up that cabal but we have no one in politics right now who seems willing or capable of addressing the issue. Even if we fix the functional pieces that are out of whack, our democracy and quality of life will decline if we do not do something about restoring true opportunity and addressing income inequality.

This malaise does not just exist in the legislative or executive branches however. For years conservatives have decried the Supreme Court of the 1960s and 1970s as a left-wing "activist court" encroaching on the right of Congress to enact the laws governing the land. But the court as composed since the late 1990s has been the most activist. They interfered with state election laws (what happened to States Rights?) quashed campaign finance laws and ruled against sensible gun laws. I ask you, how activist is that?

I am proud to be an American and consider myself fortunate to have been born in this amazing country. My birthplace has placed me, and my family, in the top percentile of the world's most fortunate. I had nothing to do with it however I do not take it for granted. That being said, I think all Americans need to be vigilant and not take our blessings for granted. Just as this article addresses our political and economic issues, we need to put America's place in the world in perspective. Most importantly, we should never stop striving to make our country the best it can be. There is constant work in maintaining the ideal of John Winthrop's "America is a shining city on a hill."

I sometimes cringe when people loudly exclaim "America is the greatest country in the world." While I believe we are a great and essential country for the defense of democracy, here are a few statistics that should give us pause – and makes us strive harder to make America the best it can be.

American Rankings in the World

Education systems – (2014) 14th

Births to women aged 15-19 – (2013) reduced from 8th to one of the lowest in developed countries

Maternal Mortality Ratio – (2015) 46th

Highest GDP per head – (2017) 19th

Inequality – adjusted human development index – (2017) 25th

Balance of payments: Current Account – (2016) Largest deficit – 1st

Government debt as a percent of GDP – (2017) 12th at 107.8

Innovation index (adoption of new technology in business & science) – (2018) 4th

Technological readiness index (economy adopting new technology) – 20th **(Not Updated)**

Total expenditures on R & D – (2018) 1st

Highest life expectancy – (2017) 42nd

Highest health spending as a percent of GDP– (2016) 1st – 31 percent higher than 2nd country Switzerland

Obesity percent of total population – (2017) 1st overall, 1st for men at 44.2 percent, 4th for women at 48.3 percent

World giving index – Top givers percent of Population – 1st at 60 percent

Defense spending – 1st (more than nine times the next highest expenditure by China)

Biggest emitters of carbon dioxide – (2017) 2nd

Renewable sources of energy as percent of electricity production – (2018) 2nd, previously 30th

Infrastructure grade, American Society of Civil Engineers – (2016) D+ (Cost to repair $2 trillion)

FEDERALISM TODAY

Written June 2013 (Updates in Bold)

Two hundred and twenty six years ago our founders met to debate and write a new constitution to replace the Articles of Confederation which were wholly inadequate in providing for the nations survival and effective operation.

After more than two centuries, we are still having some of the same debates that were argued during the years after the Convention up to the Constitution's ratification in 1789. The arguments for a stronger federal presence and diverse economy that were made by Alexander Hamilton, James Madison and John Jay comprise the Federalist Papers. The opponents were adherents to Thomas Jefferson's idea of an agrarian citizen-led Republic dominated by local and state elected officials with weak federal powers. The shifting roles and power between the federal and state governments has ebbed and flowed over the course of the last two centuries. As we enter the third century, the debate seems as alive as ever. Issues, with modern twists our founders could not have anticipated, have required every branch of our government to respond. Your view of these responses may depend on which side of the Federalist debate you identify with – Jefferson's weak federal government and a strict interpretation of the Constitution or Hamilton's strong federal government with a loose, adaptive interpretation.

Judicial

The Supreme Court in its 5-4 decision in *Gore v Bush, 2000,* in effect elected a President by denying Florida's Supreme Court the right to determine the correct time frame and date the votes had to be recounted by and which votes were legitimate. (Hanging Chads) In my mind, this is a direct violation of the separation of powers.

Cities and states have seen some of their efforts to pass their own gun control laws overturned by the Supreme Court (*District of Columbia v Heller, 2008*) and state laws now being passed in the wake of the Sandy Hook Elementary School shooting in the Newtown, CT tragedy are sure to be challenged. We are still debating the limitations of the Second Amendment but we are living in the world of modern technology with lethal weapons our founders could not have envisioned an individual or a militia possessing – assault weapons, large capacity magazines and laser-guided sights.

Perhaps most egregious of all in *Citizens United v FEC*, 2010, the court held that corporations have the same First Amendment right to free speech as an individual person. Wait a minute, you mean Exxon and Bank of America have the right to pour unlimited funds into an election for a candidate of their choice thus vastly overriding my individual vote? The founders would never have approved. Perhaps no other decision has raised the ire of both individual citizens and legal scholars who are denouncing the decision as one of the worst in the court's history. To quote Justice Stevens in his 90 page dissenting report (joined by Ginsburg, Breyer and Sotomayer), the ruling, "threatens to undermine the integrity of elected institutions across the Nation. The path it has taken to reach its outcome will, I fear, do damage to this institution." He wrote: "A democracy cannot function effectively when its constituent members believe laws are being bought and sold." Exactly!"

So the question is "How do we enhance our democracy with a balance of powers when the judiciary oversteps its bounds by interfering with legislative laws AND executive elections?

Legislative

The House of Representatives has, at current count, voted three times **(60 times up to Jan 2017)** to repeal the Affordable Care Act. The Act survived a Supreme Court challenge, not on the grounds that it should have been upheld though. The Act should have delivered a 9-0 vote that the Act was constitutional on the grounds of the federal power to regulate commerce. Instead it was decided 5-4 by Chief Justice Roberts on the power to tax thus narrowing the commerce clause —perhaps a bigger long-term problem that Congress will have to deal with in the future. Again, the choice is Jefferson's right of the individual and the state versus the right of the federal government to control its largest budget cost and provide for the general welfare of the people. Libertarians, and some Conservatives, call it the Nanny State. The preamble to the Constitution refers to it as "promote the general Welfare."

Recently our Senators failed to agree on a provision that has over 80 percent of the public's support, a comprehensive background check for all gun purchases regardless of source. It is a common sense approach to knowing who is attempting to buy a weapon and to control who receives them. Society needs some form of control over a deadly weapon. The vote was a failure, probably for a few reasons, but I believe mostly as another supposed infringement on a person's Second Amendment right; An amendment which actually states 'the right of the militia" to bear arms—not explicitly an individual right. So much for Congressional action to the 80 percent approval of the American voter to pass reasonable legislation.

Shortly before this article was written, America experienced 12 killed, 58 injured in the Aurora movie theatre shooting as well as the horror of 26 children and teachers killed by a crazed shooter using a semi-automatic weapon in their elementary school in Sandy Hook, CT. Subsequently we have continued to watch the tragedies of the Orlando nightclub and Las Vegas concert shootings – the largest mass murder in American history. Seventeen senseless murders at Marjory Stoneman Douglas High School. Where is the common-sense legislation for banning assault weapons, large capacity magazines, bump stocks, unlimited gun and ammunition sales without tracking? We have a mish mash of state laws and no comprehensive federal register of who is doing what with deadly weapons – all legislation killed by the National Rifle Association (NRA) and the members of Congress who are beholden to them.

With four percent of the population, Americans have 42 percent of the world's guns. In one year, 2016, Americans purchased an additional 27 million guns! Insanity.

As mentioned in the last column, the filibuster has been invoked by the Republican members of the Senate more than any time in history. This is a disgrace. There are so many federal judgeships and Circuit Court nominations that have not been voted on that our judiciary is seriously hampered serving the needs of justice. This is obstruction of both the executive and judicial branches. The filibuster is simply a Senate rule – it is not in the Constitution and perhaps it is time for it to be removed entirely or at least severely restricted.

Executive

The executive branch has been hampered by Congress in its efforts to implement laws already passed for financial regulation (Dodd-Frank) and health care.(Affordable Care Act). Proposed immigration reforms, dealing with long-term budget deficits and economic stimulus in the face of the Great Recession, have all been held captive to partisan interests thus preventing the progress Americans deserve.

Congress has prevented President Obama from closing Guantanamo because of their refusal to transfer captives to federal maximum security prisons and granting captives the right to face a trial in a federal court. This is a denial of a fundamental human right, to know the charges against you and trial by an impartial jury. Do Americans really believe in holding people forever without presentation of charges and granting a trial?

Congressional Republicans have refused to vote on Obama's selection for the Director of the Consumer Financial Protection Bureau and he was forced to make a recess appointment. These protections for all Americans came out of the excesses causing our near economic collapse in 2008. I simply do not understand the refusal to move forward.

A longstanding issue between the executive and legislative branches of government, the War Powers Act of 1973, is the use of the executive privilege to wage war. Obama and past presidents have ignored the law requiring Congressional approval after 60 days. We saw this most recently in Libya. I wonder what Washington, Jefferson, Madison and Hamilton would have to say about this denial of approval and the current use of Predator drone strikes against foreign citizens?

Congress however has not totally shirked its duty to oversee the executive as we have seen hearings on the Fast and Furious gun tracking fiasco, misleading information about the Benghazi Operation and now the IRS's overly aggressive scrutiny and treatment of conservative groups applying for tax-exempt status.

Thus we can see that our federal division of powers has some uphill work to do to restore the balance the founders envisioned. An activist judiciary, a dysfunctional, ineffective Congress hampered by partisanship and its own rules and an executive branch that is unable to move forward items as basic as a budget. The executive branch appears to be ineffective in its pursuit of domestic issues and too powerful in the exercise of hostilities.

Shortly after his State of the Union speech to Congress and the American people in February 2019, President Trump announced he would declare a state of emergency exists on the southern border of the United States. Further, he would appropriate money provided by Congress from existing government budgets to build a controversial wall. This is a direct violation of the separation of powers and will be challenged immediately by Congress in the courts. There is no evidence of a state of emergency on our southern border. This precedent breaking abuse of the War Powers Act must not stand—if it does, it means that a sitting president has emasculated Congress and maintains almost unlimited power.

We can take heart however. This is the 46th anniversary of the Watergate scandal and the balance of power our founders wisely gave us worked in that crisis to restore political accountability and stability.

TAKING BACK CONTROL OF THE PEOPLE'S HOUSE: END GERRYMANDERING

Written November 2013 (Updates in Bold)

Ignoring the Will of the People

Americans just experienced a spectacle and an ordeal that should have never happened – a government shutdown for 16 days and the unprecedented step (for the second time in recent years) of a Congress that threatened to refuse to raise the debt ceiling for laws and monetary expenditures they had already passed. Refusing to honor America's debt is a direct violation of the 14th Amendment. The proper way to change or correct legislation already passed is to first win elections on the basis of your policies and then debate and pass changes in the regular Congressional order of business – not by tying repeal or funding a law to the budget process or debt ceiling. Failing to raise the debt ceiling would have global economic implications that followed the loss of confidence by foreigners for the world's currency reserve. The cost of the shutdown to the American economy is estimated at $24 billion. What is perhaps worse is the loss of global confidence in our ability to lead ourselves, much less the world's economies. By the end of 2013, we hoped to avoid this manufactured crisis again on January 15th and February 7th, 2014 when the matter comes up yet again. China and Japan, hardly longtime allies, considered holding talks with other nations to depose the American dollar as the world's currency reserve. Now isn't that's a vote of no confidence in Congress and American politics?

We need to ask ourselves how politicians elected to do the work of ALL the people can so widely ignore the wishes of the majority of citizens who thought these legislative actions were not warranted? The answer is gerrymandered districts. The last redistricting process after the 2010 census allowed state legislatures to draw districts that were almost perfectly designed for the re-election of the majority House member by packing like-minded voters into absurdly drawn districts. Thus their only fear of losing an election is to lose a primary challenge. There is little need for these members to propose and support legislation that addressed the needs of a wide demographic mixture of races, ages, incomes, ideas and political persuasions. In short, there is absolutely no need for moderation. That situation subverts our democracy.

Gerrymandering, by any party, simply should not be acceptable to voters. It is a direct diminution of your vote.

Both parties are guilty of using the process to stack the deck but the extent to which it has altered voting results and changed representation in Congress is now at a whole new level of abuse. The Republican State Leadership Committee, a

Washington D.C. based political group, has sponsored a $30 million multiyear program to influence redistricting by implementing a two-pronged strategy, 1) take over state legislatures before a census is taken and, 2) redraw state and Congressional districts to their advantage. My Congressional district here in West Cary went from David Price's(D) 4th District to the 2nd District now represented by Renee Ellmers(R) from Harnett County. Ellmers just voted to keep the government shut down in the recent self-inflicted crisis. The redrawn 2nd District was quite a reach into Wake County to pack as many Republicans as possible into it. Nationally, Democrats received 1.4 million more votes in the last election for the House but Republicans control the house 234 to 201.

Regardless of which party candidate you support and the ideas you would like to see debated and enacted, it will not happen when representation is this skewed and it certainly is not supporting what makes democracy tick—moderation and compromise. In an October 4, 2013 Associated Press article, Charles Babington noted that in the last shutdown in 1995, "…79 House Republicans represented districts carried by Democrat Bill Clinton in the previous presidential election. Today, only 17 House Republicans come from districts that Obama won."

According to an article by Sam Wang, founder of the Princeton Election Consortium, in the February 3, 2013 New York Times Sunday Review Section, *The Great Gerrymander of 2012,* writing about the naïve notion that a party that wins more than half the votes should receive at least half of the seats; "Five states failed to clear even this low bar; Arizona, Michigan, North Carolina, Pennsylvania and Wisconsin... In North Carolina, where the two party House vote was 51 percent Democratic, 49 percent Republican, the average simulated delegation [a computer simulation of typical voters in the rest of the nation with the same NC statewide voter total] was seven Democrats and six Republicans. The actual outcome? [Republican redistricting] Three Democrats, ten Republicans – a split that occurred in less than one percent of simulations." In other words, extreme gerrymandering.

A lawsuit against the redistricting is currently before both the U.S. Supreme Court (SCOTUS) and the N.C. Supreme Court (after losing a lower court ruling) and the plaintiffs (NAACP, Democratic Party and individual voters) are asking Supreme Court Judge Paul Martin Newby to recuse himself from the case. Newby is reported to have received over $1 million to campaign committees supporting his re-election from the above mentioned Republican State Leadership Committee. The RSLC also supplied one of the consultants identified by GOP lawmakers as the chief architect of the new districts.

Enact NC Voters First Act

Voters do not have to sit by and watch our representation continuously be diluted, as well as politically, socially and economically misrepresented. We should prevent the politicians in the N.C. state legislature from redrawing the districts – we already know they will always act in their own best re-election interest. The State of California has in fact instituted this reform as a result of the voter referendum initiative aptly named Voters First Act. The law instituted a 14 member citizen commission to redraw Congressional, Senate, Assembly and Board of Equalization districts. The commission is composed of members from varied ethnic backgrounds and geographic locations that include five Republicans, five Democrats and four Decline to State. The commission includes educators, law professors, business and civic leaders as well as strategic consultants amongst other professions. Districts are drawn considering these criteria:

- Districts must be of equal population to comply with the U.S. Constitution.

- Districts must comply with the Voting Rights Act to ensure that minorities have an equal opportunity to elect representatives of their choice.

- Districts must be contiguous so that all parts of the district are connected to each other.

- Districts must respect the boundaries of cities, counties, neighborhoods and communities of interest, and minimize their division, to the extent possible.

- Districts should be geographically compact, that is, have a fairly regular shape.

- Where practicable each Senate District should be comprised of two complete and adjacent Assembly Districts and Board of Equalization districts shall be composed of ten complete and adjacent State Senate Districts.

- Districts shall not be drawn to favor or discriminate against an incumbent, candidate, or political party.

North Carolina citizens should follow the N.C. redistricting lawsuit closely—properly drawn districts and voter representation is at stake. California has provided the model – Independents, Republicans and Democrats, let's join together to enact a North Carolina Voters First Act to help restore some faith, accountability and representation by people who reflect a variety of sensible ideas and policies for all of the people in our great state. **As of 2018, Twenty-three states have commissions or are seeking them so progress is being made.**

Thirteen of the N.C. legislature's 2011 district maps have been ordered by the courts to be redrawn and two have them have been ruled unconstitutional as outright racial gerrymanders. In 2016 a special master redrew the maps but they were also challenged. Because the legal cases have taken so long, the districts will have to be used again for the 2018 election. For seven years the people of North

Carolina have had to live with improper representation. The SCOTUS needs to declare them what they are – extreme partisan election districts limiting our democracy. SCOTUS is expected to rule for the first time on partisan gerrymandering on cases brought by Democrats in North Carolina and Republicans in Maryland. The much anticipated ruling is expected in June 2019.

As of October 2018, N.C. House Bill 200 for a citizen impartial body to accomplish redistricting after each ten year census, has sat for over 575 days without a vote. The bill is bipartisan with 39 sponsors but the leadership refuses to take any action. North Carolina citizens need to take direct action with their elected N.C. House member to demand a vote.

DUMP THE ELECTORAL COLLEGE

Written October 2013 (Updates in Bold)

The election of a President and Vice President was a problem that the Constitutional Convention delegates struggled with mightily. While Madison and others stood strong for the people to have representation, the overriding concern centered around the balance between the representation of the states (Senate) and representation of the people (House) thus comprising a true federalist system. And of course the other motive was to agree to the three-fifths compromise to appease the southern states thus disenfranchising the slaves.

Signing the Constitution – Image by Gerd Altmann from Pixabay

Early on the convention delegates decided against a straight populist vote with the highest totals electing both offices of the executive branch. The debates continued throughout the convention and were sent to the Unresolved Issue Committee for resolution. Among the decisions they made in September, 1787 were the four year term of office with possibility of reelection, and in a compromise to the smaller states, the appointment or election of electors to indicate the vote for both President and Vice President to Congress. Representation is to be by the number of members of Congress (two Senators and X House members) based on population. This was the compromise to maintain a federalist approach to the election of the President and Vice President.

The individual states were to have control over the appointment or election of the electors and to the apportionment of the vote. After the vote debacle between Thomas Jefferson and Aaron Burr in the election of 1800 took place, during which Burr backtracked on his agreement to take the Vice Presidency, Congress and the states enacted the 12th Amendment to make each office a separate vote and ballot. The 22nd Amendment limited holding presidential office to two terms.

Today, 48 states have winner take all systems (largest vote total wins all electoral votes) with Maine and Nebraska using the Congressional District Method of apportioning the elector votes. Thus we have the modern Electoral College.

The Electoral College poses several problems causing opponents of the system to call for its outright abolishment. The elections of 1876, 1888, 2000 **and 2016** produced an Electoral College winner who did not win the popular vote. **Hillary Clinton won the popular nationwide vote by nearly three million votes. However, there were not enough "faithless electors" to intelligently select the most qualified candidate. Madison's safeguard just does not work. The result—three million disenfranchised voters.** It negates the whole notion of one man, one vote. Can we continue to call that democracy?

The system also grants the small states inordinate representation for the votes cast by their smaller populations. Based upon its population Ohio has 18 votes and Rhode Island with only 1.2 million people should have three. Rhode Island receives four electoral votes. Thus anyone in Ohio could claim tiny Rhode Island stole some of their voting influence. California, the state with the highest population, is a full ten electoral votes short it should have if the system was based on population. But it gets worse. Because we have removed the direct vote of the people, what we end up with is candidates concentrating their time and money on the *swing states only* in order to amass the highest number of electoral votes. So citizens in Nebraska, Montana or Wyoming never get to see and hear a presidential candidate in person in an election year. Instead of big ideas and solutions for national issues, candidates need

only to craft the messages that are going to reso-
nate in the swing states.

The video at this link explains the distorting
aspects of the system very succinctly:
https://youtube.com/watch?v=7wC42HgLA4k

Other issues with the Electoral College include discouraging voter turnout except in the
swing states. If a state is dominated by one party
or the other receives the same number of electoral votes it does not really matter what the voter
turnout is as opposed to a national popular vote
determining the winner. We pride ourselves in
our democracy but in most presidential elections
we do not turnout many more than 50% of the
qualified voters to the polls – the Electoral College suppresses voter turnout – not a recipe for a
healthy democracy.

**The system also hides voter disenfranchise-
ment and voting problems because all you see
are the votes of the electors.**

For example, North Carolina now, firmly in
the hands of the Republican party, just passed
one of the most regressive Voter ID and election
change laws in the country. It is widely believed
that the law will disenfranchise college students
(their college ID is now invalid) the elderly who
no longer drive and the poor – a lower voter
turnout with no effect because we still report our
15 electoral votes to Congress. **This measure
was ruled unconstitutional by the courts. Un-
deterred by legalities, the NC legislature**

placed a constitutional amendment requiring a voter ID on the ballot for the November 2018 election and the amendment passed.

What began as an attempt to maintain a federalist system and to maintain the influence of the southern states has simply morphed into a complicated system that robs every voter of their potential impact. Every argument by the proponents of keeping the Electoral College: preventing urban-centric victory, maintaining the federal character of the country and separation of powers, the supposed increase of the power of minorities and the stability of the two-party system, all seem specious defenses to me. All of these arguments together cannot make up for the loss of democratic decision-making through one person, one vote. In my opinion, it is time to abolish the Electoral College.

How might we accomplish this? A 27th Amendment is one possibility but given the current fractious political climate its passage is highly unlikely. The Every Vote Counts Amendment has languished in Congress since 2009. Another possibility is the National Popular Vote Interstate Compact (www.nationalpopularvote.com) Using the powers the constitution grants the states in selecting its electors, **12 states and the District of Columbia have already passed laws allowing their electors to grant their state votes to the winner of the national popular vote. Maryland was the first to join in 2007 and Connecticut the latest in 2018. This comprises only 172**

electoral votes, 98 electoral votes short. We need North Carolina and several other states to join the compact to reach the 270 electoral votes that are needed to effect the change.

As with campaign finance reform, a change to elect presidents with a popular vote will not occur unless the people demand it. Your vote, and mine, should count and not be buried in an obscure, out-of-date process over two centuries old and intended for only 13 states. Let's work together to make the change.

THE CORRUPTION OF CONGRESS OR: HOW I LEARNED TO START WORRYING AND HATE THE MONEY

Written July 2013 (Updates in Bold)

As Benjamin Franklin was wheeled out of the Constitutional Convention in Philadelphia a woman asked him, "Mr. Franklin what have you wrought, 'A Republic madam, if you can keep it.'"

"Thus, it is manifest that the best political community is formed by citizens of the middle class, and that those states are likely to be well-administered in which the middle class is large, and stronger if possible than both other classes..."
Quote from Aristotle *Politics*

"I believe there are more instances of the abridgement of freedom of the people by gradual and silent encroachments by those in power than by violent and sudden usurpations."
Quote from James Madison

Our Founding Fathers left no doubt where they stood in the matter of the mechanisms of governing our new nation. The people were to be in control through their elected representatives who should be wise enough to rule for the interests of the majority and the general welfare; Not elected officials acting for narrow special interests. "We the People of the United States, in Order to form a more perfect Union, establish Justice, Insure domestic Tranquility, provide for the common defence, promote the general Welfare, and secure the Blessings of Liberty to ourselves and our Posterity, do ordain and establish this Constitution for the United States of America."

That seems a long way from where We the People now stand and feel about Congress. You know it and I know it, Congress has become corrupted. We have ignored it for far too long. A small group of our citizens, and the money they contribute, have corrupted Congress and the intended working of our democracy. It is a legitimate corruption. The work of the people is not being accomplished, only the work of special interests. Neither the Right nor the Left, or anyone in between, can count on agenda items important to them being enacted if any, or part of the solution, lies in going against the special interest lobbies represented by Washington's K Street. No wonder citizen polls of Congress place their approval rating at 14 percent. **(19 percent 2017)**

Lawrence Lessig, director of Harvard's Edmond J. Safra Center for Ethics, in his book *Lesterland: The Corruption of Congress and How to End It* succinctly describes the evolution of the removal of political decisions from the hands the people to the hands of the funders and special interests. This article will discuss his major points, but you can also view his synopsis in his TED Talk at the following video link: https://youtube.com/watch?v=mw2z9lV3W1g

Lessig notes that there are in effect two elections, the money elections and the general elections. The small group of citizens that provide the funding (The Relevant Funders) for the selection of the candidates they prefer to run is the money election. Thus our choices have already been restricted for the general election. Lessig notes, "To be able to run in the voting election, one must do extremely well in the money election... The average amount raised [2012] by winning Senate candidates was $10.4 million; losing candidates $7.7 million. The average amount raised by winning House candidates was $1.6 million; losing candidates raised $774,000. Money certainly isn't the only thing that matters. But anything other than money is way, way down the list of 'things that matter.'" Lessig quotes funder statistics from 2010: 0.26 percent gave $200 or more to any Congressional candidate—about 809,229 out of our total population of 311 million. 0.05 percent gave the maximum amount of $2,400 – that is one-twentieth of the one percent, about 150,000 Americans. About the same number of people named Lester in America and thus the title of the book. Lessig says 0.00024 percent gave $100,000 or more to any combination of federal candidates, or about 750 individuals. From the 2012 Presidential election, "0.000032 percent—or 99

Americans—gave 60 percent of the individual SuperPAC money spent in the 2012 cycle."

Image by PublicDomainPNG from Pixabay

The incoming 2012 class of new freshmen Democrats were given a daily schedule by the Democratic Congressional Campaign Committee that they were expected to keep. Out of their nine hour day they were expected to spend four hours for call time – that is fundraising. The message is clear—spend most of your time fundraising leaving maybe two hours to be in Committee or on the floor. One hour was for strategic outreach thus it is possible for them to spend five hours fundraising. This is not the work of the people but courting funders and special interests.

Lessig makes three points about this political evolution:

1. The U.S. is Lesterland
2. The U.S. is worse than Lesterland. If Lester's are like the U.S. they are a dynamic group of

races, ages, sexual orientations, rich and poor. You would expect some of their decisions to benefit the public good. The U.S. is worse because as Lessig notes, "In U.S.A. land, we know what's real: Our Lester's – the Funders – don't exercise their power to serve the public good… [They] use their power to advance their own private good." If you need a good example, all you have to do is remember what happened to the financial system reforms after the crash in 2008. Most sections of the reforms that seriously addressed the major reasons for the collapse were removed from the reform bill or watered down to the point of being useless. On top of that Wall Streets' K Street friends, and our elected officials, have either refused to fund the initiatives that did pass or have delayed their implementation in Congress with sheer obstructionism. Having been on Wall Street for the crash, I knew the faults and what needed correcting and I wrote two articles about financial reform. I watched with dismay as the Congressional wrangling went on and on and provision after provision truly needed was stripped out of the legislation. To this day, derivatives are still not regulated in a transparent market as they should be.

3. In the U.S., a Lesterland-like government is a "corruption" It is legal corruption, "It is not the bad behavior of bad souls. It's the ordinary behavior of good souls within a corrupted system… Congress is filled with peo-

ple who have allowed a system of influence to develop that has corrupted the institution they have the honor to serve."

As previously mentioned, The Supreme Court (*Citizens United v FEC, 2000)* has now made the influence of the Funders even more powerful. We need an amendment to the Constitution to over-turn this decision as soon as possible. We don't even have the FEC to monitor election laws. As the April 14, 2013 New York Times editorial noted, "It is an open scandal in Washington that the Federal Election Commission is completely ossified as the referee and penalizer of abuses in national politics." The article went to describe Carl Rove's Crossroads GPS outrageous response to an FEC inquiry about spending, stating, [the inquiries] 'are unnecessary' but if they keep coming it will offer the same unrevealing re-sponse.

So what do We the People do to regain their rightful place in determining our laws and poli-cies? We have to place ourselves back in the prime position as both funders and voters. If we do not do that, all the structural changes such as getting rid of the Electoral College, Amendment for Citizens United or eliminating the filibuster, will not make any difference. All of us working together need to force this change through con-certed action, participation and financial support to organizations that are working to implement campaign finance reforms. We have to give Con-gressional members a way out of the Skinner box of relying on the current fundraising mechanisms to remain in office or entering the revolving door to work for K Street lobbyists where they obtain obscene pay raises. We have to place citizen servants back in Congress.

TIME TO END THE FILIBUSTER

Written August 2013 (Updates in Bold)

When George Washington brought Thomas Jefferson back from France to serve as Secretary of State, Jefferson asked Washington why he had supported the Senate as a second chamber. "Why," asked Washington in response, "did you pour that coffee into your saucer?" "To cool it." answered Jefferson. "Even so," said Washington, "we pour legislation into the senatorial saucer to cool it."

Quote from *A More Perfect Union: The Making of the United States Constitution* by William Peters

The Founders envisioned the Senate as a more deliberative body that could reconsider legislation passed by the House. However, they did not envision the emergence of political parties. That occurred with the debate for the ratification of the Constitution, with the Hamiltonian Federalists and Jeffersonian Democratic-Republicans emerging. They certainly did not expect the current gridlocked two-party system that has become so partisan and dysfunctional that the work of the people is not being accomplished. Unfortunately the use of a Senate rule, the filibuster, has become a major part of the impediments to executive and legislative progress.

Here are a few examples of how far our political system has eroded:

- "The single most important thing we want to achieve is for President Obama to be a one-term president." Senator Mitch McConnell, October 23, 2010. Isn't that a great way as a minority leader to reach across the aisle and try to accomplish the work of the people? Rep. John Boehner's message to his House caucus this week before the August recess stated that their job is "to fight Washington" They are Washington!
- Holding the debt ceiling (the full faith and credit of the U.S. government) and proposed annual budgets hostage. As of today we are down to nine days left in this session to pass a budget. **(2019 – we are in the 30th day of a shutdown over border security)**
- Actually allowing the Congressional gun-to–the-head sequester process (automatic spending cuts) to go into effect. Compromise could not be found even hiding under the bed!
- Refusing, through unprecedented use of the filibuster, to vote on executive and judicial nominees.

Ezra Klein in a February 6, 2013 Washington Post editorial quoted comments by political scientist Greg Koger. "American democracy isn't only very different today than the Founders ever imagined, it's very different today than it was 50 years ago… Over the last 50 years, we have added a new veto point in American politics. It used to be the House, the Senate and the president and now it's the House, the president, the Senate majority and the Senate minority. Now you need to get past four veto points to pass legislation. That's a huge change of constitutional priorities. But it's been done, almost unintentionally, through procedural strategies of party leaders."

There are currently about 85 circuit and district court seats that are vacant. This is double the number at this point in the Bush administration. 28 of these vacancies have been declared judicial emergencies because of the length of time they have been unfilled and the case workload. The average wait for Bush's circuit and district court confirmation was 35 days, it is 148 for Obama's circuit, and 102 days for district court confirmation. These nominations deserve votes now and Obama owes it to the people and the court system to make nominations now for every other vacant seat. The media needs to inform Americans of the status of all the nominations and hold everyone's feet to the fire – that is their job.

We have seen Senate Republicans filibuster presidential appointments so that President Obama had to make recess appointments of Richard Cordray as head of the Consumer Financial Protection Bureau and four members to the National Labor Relations Board. Gina McCarthy as head of EPA has also been held up. Decorum in the Senate hit bottom when junior Republicans tried to filibuster nominations for national security posts. These posts in the past had always received bipartisan support.

> **Unfortunately the use of the filibuster has become a major impediment to progress. In the past it was used very sparingly, now it is used as a tool of obstruction with seemingly little concern for invoking it.**

In a report for CNN, Julian Zelizer states, "But the number of filibusters has escalated, and they have been far more willing to use the tactic than their opponents. Since 2007, the Senate Historical Office has shown, Democrats have had to end Republican filibusters more than 360 times, a historic record... Senators have also employed additional tactics such as anonymous holds, whereby senators can secretly prevent action on a bill and nobody can know who is responsible."

Many people believe it is time to reform the filibuster with some calling for its outright elimination. Reid and McConnell have spent hours excoriating each other over the issue in the past month. Reid finally announced that he had the votes to implement the so called "Nuclear Option" by changing the Senate rule to end a filibuster with 51 votes rather than 60. Reid explained this was done only to move the stalled 85 federal judiciary appointments and not intended for Supreme Court nominees.

So where are we at today? The Senate, thanks in large part to Sen. John McCain's efforts, recently reached a compromise that allows the filibuster to exist in its present form. In return,

Obama will get his executive nominees confirmed.

This was really another instance of politicians kicking the can down the road because they did not apply the compromise deal to the judicial nominations. The most crucial of these vacancies are the three nominations to the U.S. Court of Appeals for the D.C. Circuit. It is the second most important court in the land because of its rulings on national security and federal regulations. We could be right back to the Nuclear Option for these nominations in a few months. **(Harry Reid did exercise the nuclear option)**

In February 2016, in an unprecedented move, Sen. McConnell and the Republicans let it be known that they would not hear or confirm any justice until the country elected a new president that November. Both parties are guilty of these abuses that fly in the face of decorum, seeking legislative compromise and honestly approving the president's choice of a qualified candidate to the nation's highest court with a majority.

We will have to wait and see if "saving" the filibuster is a positive action or if its use will continue to block executive and legislative progress. One thing is certain, it will not be a positive development if it continues to be used so frequently for pure political obstruction. Unfortunately only the Senate can change its own rules but pressure from constituents to reduce its use with the promise that we will hold them accountable at the ballot box could make a difference. It

is the only thing they seem to pay attention to –
losing their job.

WE ARE GOING BACKWARD: APATHY, VOTING RIGHTS AND THE MEDIA

Written December 2013 (Updates in Bold)

"The cause of America is, in great measure, the cause of all mankind. Many circumstances have, and will arise, which are not local, but universal, and through which the principles of all lovers of mankind are affected..."- Thomas Paine *Common Sense*

To date this column has covered several topics the citizens of America should discuss and perhaps support to revitalize our now moribund and dysfunctional political system. The articles have included: A review of the legislative, executive and judicial dysfunction we have experienced since 2000 and America's world-ranking in several areas, campaign finance reform and monetary corruption, ending the filibuster, revoking the Electoral College and the harmful effects of gerrymandering.

This fact is the 800 pound gorilla in the room. With the exception of four presidential elections (1952, 1960, 1964 and 1968) the percentage of those eligible to vote, who actually cast a vote, has not exceeded 60 percent. We simply cannot have a vibrant, active and participatory democracy when over 40 percent of our citizens are disengaged from their most important obligation to society. That astounds me! Yet we have been cruising along with this low turnout for so long that this is now the normal state of affairs. The media does not even discuss, as one of our major issues, the missing 40 percent.

What are we to think about this widespread apathy? We hear an endless litany of excuses. Is it "my vote does not matter," "the politicians have it all rigged already," "business and Wall Street own the country," I can't be bothered to take time out of my day." Apathy on this scale prohibits our democracy from moving forward. We need to reinstitute civics classes in all of the nation's high schools to educate future voters about the power and importance of their individual votes and how our local, state and national governments work. The civics classes should be taught alongside U.S. History I and II courses typically taken in $9^{th}/10^{th}$ and 11th grades.

Madison studied the failure of past democracies and believed that an educated citizenry, especially in civics and our constitution, was the best way to ensure against "crafty and

dangerous encroachments on the public liberty... A popular government, without popular information, or the means of acquiring it, is but a Prologue to a Farce or a Tragedy; or perhaps both."

So while we have a huge number of missing voters, do you think the states have been making it easier to vote? No, at least 11 states have been busy enacting more restrictive laws that they claim "protect" the integrity of the process. Bunk! These changes as explained in the next paragraph, are a solution in search of a problem. Voter fraud is not an issue of any statistical significance.

Sadly, North Carolina was part of the movement. In my opinion, we have taken a large step backwards. Do not forget that North Carolina had 42 counties that were covered by the recently nullified Section Four of the Voting Rights Act because of past voting abuses. The Justice Department agrees with the critics of the new law and has sued the state to halt some of the changes using a remaining section of the Voting Rights Act not struck down by the current Supreme Court. Those changes are: requiring a photo ID to vote, the shortening of early voting from 17 days to 10, the elimination of same-day registration during early voting and restrictions on counting some provisional ballots. In addition, a N.C. voter can no longer vote a straight party ticket, the order a candidate appears on a ballot has changed from the party with the most registered voters in the state (Democrats) to the party with the Governor in office – a blatant political change. Just when we should be taking steps to increase public financing of elections, the new law removes the $3 check-off box for public financing on tax returns. The money was doled out on the basis of the most registered voters—another benefit lost to Democrats.

Speaking in 1965, President Lyndon Baines Johnson directly addressed the forces who had restricted voting rights and in support of the Voting Rights Act. He instructed them, "Open your polling places to all your people. Allow men and women to register and vote whatever the color of their skin. Extend the rights of citizenship to every citizen of this land... There is no constitutional issue here. The command of the Constitution is plain."

I really miss the late Tim Russert from NBC's Meet the Press. It seems to me that in this age of 24/7 TV, cable and radio news coupled with the ubiquitous internet, we have more opportunity than ever before to educate and enlighten ourselves. So what is the problem? In the fractured and politically polarized world of today I have found very few outlets, and the journalists who work for them, who work hard to discover and discuss the facts in the effort to reveal the truth. While politicians will always seek the spotlight to spin their message, people like Tim Russert held everyone's feet to the fire when misstatements, half-truths and outright incorrect statements were made. With few exceptions, I have not seen that questioning and search for accuracy occur on the main outlets.

Image by engine akyurt from Pixabay

Just last week Ted Cruz the junior Senator from Texas came on CNN and spoke out (a McCarthy like diatribe really) against the Affordable Care Act. During the statement he said "millions of people had lost their jobs because of Obamacare." The journalist (can I still call them that?) did not stop him and even question that number. I was infuriated. The job loss estimates are all over the place from net effect gains in jobs to a loss of 800,000 jobs – the highest number I could find in my research. The truth, as usual, probably lies somewhere in the middle – at any rate it is a far cry from "millions." Allowing blatantly incorrect information to pass unquestioned is a denial of journalistic integrity.

A 2017 University of Pennsylvania Leonard Davis Institute study stated "In summary,

with only one exception, the literature pub-
lished to date finds virtually no effect of the
ACA on employment, hours of work, ESI of-
fers, job mobility, or wages in the first two
years."

We are in big trouble if we allow unwar-
ranted statements by politicians, pundits, lobbyists or anyone else to go unchallenged. Facts
matter and the search for truth is the path that
should lead us to the actions we take to resolve
our issues and problems. I thought that was the
job of all journalists. In 1807 President Jefferson
wrote, "The man who never looks into a newspa-
per is better informed than he who reads them,
inasmuch as he who knows nothing is nearer to
truth than he whose mind is filled with false-
hoods and errors."

In a recent Nation of Change.org article the
group Media Matters spoke out about the intense
2012 climate change events, "The Sunday shows
spent less than eight minutes on climate
change…Most of the politicians quoted [on ABC
& NBC] were Republican presidential candidates, including Rick Santorum, who went unchallenged when he called global warming 'junk
science'… In four years, Sunday shows have not
quoted a single scientist on climate change." The
corporate controlled media of today is simply not
serving its intended role as a watchdog for society.

Shortly after the 2016 election data from
tracking firm mediaQuant found, "[Trump] in
FREE media…received $5.6 billion through-

out the entirety of his campaign, more than Hillary Clinton, Bernie Sanders, Ted Cruz, Paul Ryan and Marco Rubio combined."

Rather than stick to facts, analysis, presenting various views, demanding explanations of false statements, the corporate media during the entire campaign took the money and ran for the rating increases/advertising revenue due to Trump's daily Twitter outrages. In my opinion, the corporate media is a major reason why we have the most incompetent and autocratic president in American history.

But take heart – there are reliable sources available. The internet has many corporate free sources and The Corporation for Public Broadcasting (PBS & NPR) was founded for this very reason – to provide the public with the best indepth and thoughtful information available. We can seek out experts known for their journalistic integrity in print (newspapers, magazines and scholarly journals) as well as the internet.

We need a press that, rather than deferring to authority or pleasing corporate owners, challenges authority for truthfulness at every turn. America and the world have tremendous obstacles to face – we need an independent press to provide the facts and push for solutions. As the old saying goes, "Information is power."

After being bullied and lambasted by Donald Trump for 2 ½ years as "fake news" the press (print, TV, radio and internet) has finally started fulfilling its duty of rigorous questioning and reporting. As citizens we need to monetarily support print publications as well as public television and radio to ensure we are receiving the vital news stories of the day.

INEQUALITY: LIFE IN AMERICA TODAY

Written January 2014 (Updates in Bold)

Left Behind

725,000 (7 percent) North Carolina households live in poverty [Family of four income $25,750 or less](NC Policy Watch 2018)

Boone, NC – 58% live below poverty line

Clay County, GA – 42 percent live below the poverty line

Montgomery, AL and Shreveport, LA – 24 percent live below the property line

Ziebach County, SD – 40 percent live below the poverty line

Image by lannyboy89 from Pixabay

Pope Francis, one of the world's foremost leading advocates for human rights and equality, he caused a stir with his recent exhortation against rising inequality and the myth of trickle-down economics. He stated, "Some people continue to defend trickle-down theories which assume that economic growth, encouraged by a free market, will inevitably succeed in bringing about greater justice and inclusiveness in the world. This rich people friendly take on the world has never been confirmed by the facts."

He went on to make these additional points:

- We need to reject the notion of absolute autonomy of markets and to challenge the market rules that have made us staggeringly unequal.
- Wealth works best when it is spread around. "We must say 'Thou Shalt Not' to an economy of exclusion and inequality."
- Inequality endangers all of us, not just the poor.
- We are tearing our social fabric, "The worship of the ancient golden calf has returned in a new and ruthless guise."

In February 2007 I wrote about the trickle-down myth in a review of the book, *The American Dream vs. The Gospel of Wealth: The Fight for a Productive Middle-Class Economy*. The article is still a relevant read. (Appendix)

Here are some startling statistics about life in America today. We know inequality has affected all of us, we see it in our communities and we have watched it happen all across America for years. It is now a huge social, economic and moral issue. Politicians have only provided us useless sound bite promises and supposed support for the middle class when they are at home. Many do not even hold town hall meetings anymore, will speak only on conference calls or at friendly chamber meetings or fundraisers. They are adept at avoiding hearing what their constituents really think. When they return to Washington they enact laws that mainly benefit the rich. Policy for the majority has been hijacked for the benefit of the few. Like it or not, we have already had a class war and the wealthy have won.

- Share of national income going to the top one percent of earners: U.S. 1970 – eight percent, U.S. 2008 – 18 percent. Bottom 50 percent of taxpayers by contrast have only 13 percent of income. *New York Times reporting IRS data.*

- **Congressional Budget Office reported percent change in income gains from 1979 – 2014 – Top one percent 228 percent, Middle 60 percent 42 percent.**

- One percent of earners effective tax rate in 1967 – 54 percent. Effective tax rate in 2012 – 23 percent. The richest 400 Americans have more wealth than the bottom 150 million combined. *Robert Reich, Nation of Change.*

- **Minimum federal & NC 2018** wage – $7.25, **only $510 above the annual federal poverty threshold for a family of two**—a livable hourly wage is considered to be closer to $15.00. **Growth in average 2017 wages if it had grown with wages of typical worker would equal $11.62 per hour, if it had grown with productivity of workers would equal $19.33.**

- Private sector labor force covered by union contracts **2017—10.7 percent,** 7.0 percent 2012, 20.1 percent 1983, Nearly 40 percent 1952.

- Chance that citizens between the ages of 25-60 will experience at least one year below the official poverty line – 40 percent. *Professor Mark Rank, Chasing the American Dream.*

- Growth of poverty City vs Suburban – Suburban poverty growth 2000-2010 – 53 percent, City – 23 percent. *Brookings Institution, Confronting Suburban Poverty in America.*

- For African-American children, the 2012 poverty rate reported was 37.4 percent for 2011. The rate for Hispanic children was 34.1 percent. For Non-Hispanic, White children the rate was 12.5 percent. [A huge racial disparity.] *Census Bureau.*

- Average pay of CEO's at 102 major companies in 1970s – $1.2 million, average $9 million in 2002 or about 367 times the pay of the average worker. *Federal Reserve.* – **$15.6 million in 2017, 271 times average worker of $58,000.**

- 2008 (financial economic crash) pay of hedge fund managers – David Tepper $4 billion, George Soros $3.3 billion. Highest paid 2012 CEO – McKesson's John Hammergren at $131 million. *Forbes* **2017 Broadcom's Hock Tan $103.2 million.**

- Amount of wealth transfer to America's top earners from Reagan tax cuts since 1980s – $3 trillion. Amount of transfer from Bush tax cuts to top one percent—$1 trillion. *Hedrick Smith, Who Stole the American Dream.*

- Bush tax cut for middle-income families – $1,180, top one percent $58,000.

- **Obama gave stimulus tax cuts in 2009 to save the cratering economy and also made Bush's tax cuts permanent in 2010 but increased the inheritance tax.**

- **Trump's 2017 tax cut did not benefit the middle class and once again sold the discredited trickle down economic theory to Americans—the tax cut will pay for itself by stimulating the economy and create more jobs. Wrong – CBO reports in October, 2018 that the federal budget deficit**

will equal $779 billion. (See next chapter on Debt)

- Reaching the so-called American Dream – Equal Opportunity. The U.S. places ninth out of the ten peer developed countries behind Australia, Canada, Denmark and even the United Kingdom. *Foreign Policy Quarterly.*

- **2015 Milken Institute Global Equal Opportunity Index places the United States 19th in its rankings.**

How did we come so far from labor and management sharing the fruits of income brought about by productivity gains in the 1950s and 60s to the current Winner-Take-All economy that largely benefits only the executives and shareholders? There has been a relentless effort to reduce wages and move American jobs wherever that could be accomplished. The resultant labor and productivity gains go straight to the top percentile.

Was it inevitable global economic integration, technology or lowered educational achievement that has devastated our middle-class? No, the largest single cause of the decline of our middle-class and the growth of large income disparities are the decisions made by the politicians in Washington, D.C.

Beginning in the 1970s business leaders and owners systematically organized and increased their lobbying of Congress for corporate friendly tax, regulation and accounting policies that had previously acted to ensure a fair distribution of economic rewards. If you are interested in a detailed account of this transformation there are two authors who outline the changes and their implications in their books: Hedrick Smiths *Who Stole the American Dream* and Jacob Hacker and Paul Pierson's *Winner Take All Politics.* As Hacker notes, these political changes caused, "A huge transfer of income to the top, tax cuts precisely targeted to the top. We call them economic smart bombs."

Prescriptions for Change: A New American Renaissance and Social Contract

"Today, our most important task is to restart this virtuous cycle of invention and manufacturing…We need to create at least 20 million jobs in the next decade to offset the effects of the recession and to address our $500 billion trade deficit in manufactured goods." From *Who Stole the American Dream,* Susan Hockfield, President, Massachusetts Institute of Technology.

Andrew Grove, former CEO of Intel, has proposed a financial tax on every Wall Street transaction with the funds to be used for rebuilding our manufacturing base and helping new technologies scale up manufacturing. His point is that we should not be losing the manufacturing of the technologies (and thus the research and development lead in that technology) that we invent or lead the world in – examples are solar panels (lost to China) and Magnetic Levitation (Mag-

Lev) high speed rail transportation (Germany). Grove states, "Not only did we lose an untold number of jobs, we broke the chain of experience that is so important in technological evolution. Abandoning today's 'commodity' manufacturing can lock you out of tomorrow's emerging industry."

In short we need a public-private partnership engaged in implementing a new Marshall Plan for America – a new social contract requiring cooperation not conflict and certainly not a winner-take-all philosophy.

> **Washington needs to grant the tax changes and credits to spur investment in infrastructure, new technologies, green energy and research and development. To assist the movement, states need to enact Buy America First content laws.**

Hedrick Smith's book offers ten sound solutions to restoring fairness and equality for our citizens and suggestions for aspects of a Marshall Plan. Major suggestions include a simplified progressive tax code for both individuals and corporations. It calls for the removal of loopholes and tax advantages that allow avoidance of taxes and increasing the capital gains tax, taxing stock options granted executives and repatriating corporate funds parked overseas.

I would add to all of this that we have to increase our support for education at all levels and to take direct steps to reduce the cost of a college education and improve our international test standings. We are going to need all the highly educated people we can graduate for a new, fairer economy.

In 1968 Robert Kennedy appealed for justice stating "Our whole nation is degraded by wrenching poverty amidst astonishing wealth...[Those born under the most comfortable conditions] have a responsibility to others less well off. [Accommodating inequality and deprivation] ignores our common humanity and claims to civilization alike."

All of this will not happen unless we take to the streets like we did in the 1960s. Keep the Moral Mondays [in NC] and Occupy protest movements going and help make the turnouts even larger. Thoughtful people are going to have to force the change – Congress, corporations and the wealthy will not do it on their own. We the people (left, moderate & right) need to come together and work to restore democracy for all our citizens.

AUTOCRACY, TRUMP AND OUR INSTITUTIONS

Written March 2019

"Propaganda is where a demagogue plays pedagogue and starts a monologue to leave their audience agog." -Stewart Stafford

The Reality Distortion Field

I found it difficult to know where to even begin this chapter. Since the election of Donald Trump in 2016, the mores and workings of our democracy have been sorely tested. It remains to be seen if the safeguards and divisions of power our founders instituted will hold up under the onslaught.

While autocracy has seen a resurgence across the world with leaders in Hungary, Poland, the Philippines and right wing political movements in Germany and France gaining support, few of us ever expected it to also occur in America. As a people, we were too inattentive, some allowed themselves to succumb to targeted fake news, and voters in their economic and political frustration elected an individual who is spectacularly unqualified to hold the position of the President of the United States and leader of the free world.

The actions of Donald Trump, before election as president and afterword, are too numerous to elucidate here so I will focus on the most grievous. They will not be necessarily in order of occurrence.

Morality

At the top of my list is the moral outrage we should all feel at the murder of Jamal Khashoggi. He was a permanent American resident and journalist for the Washington Post. Our own CIA states he was brutally murdered and then dismembered in the Saudi Turkish Embassy at the direction of Mohammed bin Salman (MBS) the Crown Prince of Saudi Arabia. Turkey has provided our intelligence agencies incontrovertible evidence about the crime. Trumps' reaction – "well maybe he (MBS) did it or not, we don't know." We need to protect American jobs and the Saudi's are crucial to stability on the Middle East. Yes Mr. President, we do know he was responsible and you choose to look the other way. America differentiates itself by our reliance on the rule of law and no individual or country should be immune from civilized laws of decency, morality and criminality. The Saudi's must be held accountable. As with the now famous Vladimir Putin Helsinki press conference in which Trump denied Russian interference in our 2016 election, Trump has once again thrown all of our intelligence agencies under the bus and chosen to believe an autocratic ruler's obvious denial.

The GOP, for their own political expediency, have refused to place checks on Trump and halt the decline of the America's standing in the world. They are complicit in this decline.

But the question is, why are the Saudi's still our allies? The big obstacle has long since been removed—we no longer need the oil. Saudi Wahabbi radical Islamic ideology allowed and enforced by the monarchy (their deal with the devil) has been spreading hatred through its madrasa's for many years. Fifteen of the nineteen 9/11 hijackers were Saudi and it was the home of bin Laden.

Before murdering Khashoggi, the Crown Prince (MBS) had the temerity to kidnap the Lebanese Prime Minister. We are allowing them to use American made weapons for the indiscriminate killing of civilians in Yemen. Our strategy of needing the Saudi's to counter the Iranians for regional stability is now so morally flawed that it should be reconsidered by Congress and the State Department. Ask yourself, how long should we keep taking sides between Sunnis and Shia who have been killing each other since 632AD?

We all know the answer – Money, Oil and Politics. Every modern American president and Congress has kowtowed to the Kingdom. The real politic of the time, at a minimum, requires that America now yank the Saudi chain and get them back in line. Since Trump has not taken action, Congress is fulfilling its duty and is now meeting to discuss action against Saudi Arabia. Mohammed bin Salman absolutely cannot represent the Kingdom as Crown Prince and negotiate with world powers. Additionally, we must require them to cease the embargo of our ally Qatar, delay further arms sales and revoke their use of American made weapons in Yemen.

In November 2018 Congress did invoke sanctions against the Saudis as well as the Magnitsky Act which will give Trump 120 days to determine a violation of human rights by a foreign leader. To show how much the Saudis are worried about their relations with America, they recently reshuffled their key Cabinet posts and left the Crown Prince (MBS) in place with all of his ministry and official duties intact! President Trump has refused to file the required Magnitsky determination by the 120 day deadline. Another direct challenge to Congress.

In November the American people spoke and the GOP lost the majority in the House of Representatives. We can all hope that this rebalancing of power will return some semblance of morality at home and abroad as well as support for our institutions and what America represents.

North Korea
Barack Obama told Donald Trump during the transition that his greatest concern for our national security was dealing with the threat Kim

Jong-un posed in North Korea. With his usual, this is just another real estate negotiation bluster, Trump proceeded to threaten the world's most unpredictable dictator on Twitter and on television with total annihilation (my button is bigger than your button) and calling him "little rocket man." He then granted Un the thing he wanted most, a direct meeting with an American president. The summit, and any subsequent ones, are likely to produce virtually any verifiable agreement we could ever count on. Kim is playing Trump like a violin. Good for the cameras and Celebrity Apprentice but worthless to any real progress.

As recounted in Bob Woodward's recent book *Fear,* Trump has continued to press the Cabinet and staff to produce an order for his signing revoking the KORUS (U.S. – So. Korean) trade pact over a mere small trade deficit and ordering the withdrawal of American soldier's dependents. Economic advisor, Gary Cohn, Chief of Staff John Kelly and Secretary of Defense Jim Mattis all informed him that the trade action was inconsequential and the pact was actually in our interest. Most importantly, the withdrawal of dependents would be viewed by North Korea as preparation for war. A devastating war that there was no viable scenario to execute without huge loss of life, Trump balked. He then later again requested a directive for the trade action be placed on his desk for signature. At least twice Cohn or Rob Porter, White House Staff Secretary, upon seeing the prepared directive, removed it from the Resolute desk in the Oval Office – out of sight, out of mind. He simply has no understanding of the implications of his actions in any sphere. This narcissistic, uninformed and impetuous man has now become our own biggest security threat.

International Relations

While seemingly respecting the likes of Vladimir Putin and Kim Jong-un for being tough leaders, this president has berated our long standing alliances and trade pacts. He has blindsided the leaders and members of the G7 and NATO with concerns over who will pay for the Alliance. They have previously pledged higher contribution amounts and are working to achieve the targets– no one needed his bluster. He has individually insulted the Australian Prime Minister Malcolm Turnbull and questioned the wisdom of France's Emmanuel Macron and Britain's Theresa May.

On the trade front he has forced the renegotiation of NAFTA and we are not sure how this will benefit America. He and Chairman Xi Jinping of China keep escalating the amount of trade sanctions against each other. No one really wins a trade war. Trump infuriated his Chief Economic Advisor Gary Cohn for his lack of understanding of basic economics and the effects trade wars have on the average American and corporations. Cohn finally gave up and resigned.

Our alliances and support for free trade across the world have brought European peace and economic integration for over 75 years. Additionally, the Third World has also seen tremendous development and progress in lifting millions out of poverty. The return for the United States is the largest economy in the world and the ability to have the world's most sophisticated and capable military. If it ain't broke, don't fix it!

World leaders are thinking "What will he do next?" Trump has absolutely lost the faith of our most critical allies and we will continue to see them shun him. They will begin to make their own decisions for their economic activity and security regardless, and in spite of, ill-considered Trump proposals.

Lies, Fear and Incompetence

As of December 2018 the Washington Post Fact Checker has tallied Trump spewing 7,546 false (lies) or misleading statements! While adopting the long practiced GOP strategy of deflecting accurate analysis of economic and political issues toward social issues, Trump has ramped up the Us versus Them rhetoric to new levels with wildly misleading or outright false claims. His aim is stoke fear and anger against many of our own citizens (Women, Latino, LGBTQ), immigrants (murders and rapists), the press (fake news, revoking press passes) and our courts (any of the many legal decisions that have already gone against him). It doesn't stop there...he attacks his own Cabinet and staff members, announces firings or resignations before the person even knows about it or has requested it be made public, all with the ubiquitous Tweet. No consideration or common decency to people who supported and served him and attempted to keep him and America out of harm's way.

While we are now used to the media telling us when we wake up in the morning about the latest 3amTwitter storm from Trump, in the beginning I questioned what is this man doing up all night instead of getting the much need rest to handle the rigors of the world's most demanding job? By all accounts he does not even get to the Oval Office until 11am or later and who knows what he is doing while he spends a record amount of "Executive Time."

His first task every day is to receive the daily intelligence briefing. Because of his chronic inattention and refusal to read any document at length, the national security briefer has had to provide bullet points and read them to him. Does this make you feel safer?

His administration has been chaotic from the beginning. As Michael Lewis reported to us in a series of articles for Atlantic Magazine, the detailed and critical information provided by the Obama administration for the transition of each agency was never read. The Departments of Energy (guardian of our nuclear arsenal), Agriculture (food safety, FDA) and EPA staff waited for many days after the inauguration – no Trump transition staff arrived. When they finally did arrive they were not interested in the critical functions or who had expertise and who headed which function. They wanted the info on what Obama implemented so they could begin to dismantle it. The professional staffers at these agencies were completely dismayed and many simply quit government service. This has been a tremendous loss of expertise, a loss for the American people.

Institutions

Trump has had the highest turnover of Cabinet and White House staff in the first two years of any president in modern history. The exposure of their corruption forced out some (so much for draining the swamp) but most simply were infuriated by his uninformed statements, inability to learn, tirades, being dismissed and ridiculed in front of others, trying to cover for him after a policy decision was made and that he changed it in a public statement. They were exhausted by the stress and chaos. This is the operation of our government not the set of a television show!

The most prominent White House staffing losses that should concern all of us are the resignations of Chief of Staff John Kelly and Secretary of Defense James Mattis. The last two bulwarks against chaos and attempting to implement intelligent policy are no longer present. As one media outlet noted, "the guardrails are gone." Trump arbitrarily decided to withdraw from Syria falsely claiming that ISIS was defeated. The U.S. has a small footprint there (2,200 troops) but they are important to keep the alliance together and to protect the Kurds our staunchest ally. Trump compounded the insult to the military, and Mattis personally, by announcing on Twitter he would also withdraw one-half of our troops in Afghanistan. Most observers say we are now less safe here at home and this is just adding additional damage to our alliances. The action also emboldens Putin and the murderous Hafez Assad in Syria. Putin is playing Trump like a violin.

Mattis promptly resigned stating "We must do everything possible to advance an international order that is most conducive to our security, prosperity and values, and we are strengthened in this effort by the solidarity of our alliances."

Other institutions have held up fairly well under the onslaught of attacks. Courts have issued constitutional rulings, the media has continued to report the news and seek answers from the parties involved. A court ruling restored the White House pass to Jim Acosta after being revoked by Trump.

However hidden from us are the workings of the various Cabinet level departments and whether or not they are being properly administered. The EPA has had its Clean Air and Clean Water rule standards reduced by the administration. Interior Secretary Ryan Zinke has had to resign due to corruption allegations but not before he had already caused damage—Federal Recreation Lands have been reduced in size to allow development. They are some of our greatest treasures. Don't look for further health or land use protections until Trump, these Cabinet members and their staff's are no longer in office.

Betsy DeVos at Education is quietly diverting funding from public education in favor of charter schools that have unproven educational attainment track records. This reduces support for one of the institutions that made America great – our system of public schools.

With John Kelly, H.R. McMaster and James Mattis no longer in the White House, and only the "Yes" men and women left, we are probably correct in assuming that there are no longer any adults left to deflect or stop his uneducated, rash and impetuous decisions. How will this end?

Fini

The Mueller investigation into Russian interference, potential collusion and obstruction of justice has been completed with apparently no recommendation for future action. All we have received is Attorney General William Barr's 4 page summary. However, the American people, and Congress, deserve to receive the entire report and all the evidence that was gathered. Every Trump family business, foundation, campaign and inaugural committee is under investigation in various court jurisdictions. We already know that the payoffs to the two women Trump had illicit affairs with are felony campaign violations. I believe Trump has already violated the high crimes and misdemeanors as well as the emoluments clause for impeachment our founders placed in the constitution. The high crimes clause was a well-known English law phrase that had been in use since the 13th century for the purpose of removing officials who abused their office, appointed corrupt officials or were themselves incompetent. The phrase was so well understood by George Mason and James Madison and others that it was not even discussed for very long at the Constitutional Convention. The emoluments law suit is ongoing at this time in Washington D.C.

In Yoni Applebaum's article published in the March 2019 issue of Atlantic, *Impeach Donald Trump,* points out that Congress needs to serve as its intended check on the executive branch and fully investigate possible impeachment. He quotes E.P. Whipple from an 1866 Atlantic article concerning the impeachment of Andrew Johnson, "The president of the United States has so singular a combination of defects for the office of a constitutional magistrate, that he could have obtained the opportunity to misrule the nation only by a visitation of Providence. Insincere as well as stubborn, cunning as well as unreasonable, vain as well as ill-tempered, greedy of popularity as well as arbitrary in disposition, veering in his mind as well as fixed in his will, he unites in his character the seemingly opposite qualities of demagogue and autocrat…[Johnson] is egotistic to the point of mental disease… and become the prey of intriguers and sycophants."

History does repeat itself.

The House of Representatives needs to immediately begin staffing up the judiciary and intelligence committees to gather testimony and evidence from all the relevant party's regarding impeachment. While we do not want to take this action lightly, it may be the only way to bring Trump under control and restore power to the legislative branch. This presidency must at the very least be responsibly controlled by the legislative branch.

Every voter needs to weigh in with their member of the House of Representatives, and ultimately the Senate, and ask themselves, how in good conscience can they allow the perils this man poses to the functioning of our democracy and institutions to continue? Trumps lies, his incompetence and unstable personality are a constant threat to the workings of our republic.

Our elected representatives should take action on our behalf... if they do not, and that is in considerable doubt, then we the people, need to do it at the ballot box in 2020.

GETTING INVOLVED: ACTIONS YOU CAN TAKE

Climate Change

If you would like to get actively involved in the world's most pressing issue, listed below are four organizations that are taking action on climate change:

- **350.org** founded by Bill McKibben who has been an activist since 1988 and published *The End of Nature*. There are chapters in 189 countries.
- **Sierra Club** which has recently taken a more activist protest role.
- **Greenpeace** with a focus on actions directly confronting dangers to our ocean habitats.
- **Union of Concerned Scientists** focuses on sound scientific sustainability and climate change strategies.

Debt: America's Economic Deficits

The Concord Coalition is a non-partisan group founded to educate Americans about the facts of our federal debt and is a chief action agent for sustainable federal spending that protects future generations. Visit www.concordcoalition.org.

End Gerrymandering

With the 2020 elections nearing and the resulting redrawing of districts imminent, the most important action we can take is to find out the status of a citizen commission for redistricting in your state. We must remove this process from the hands of state politicians who will always act in their own self-interest and not in the interest of democracy.

- If your state does not have a citizen commission, find out the status of any bill already introduced and get behind its passage. Call your House and Senate reps and tell them you want its passage. Organize your friends – Call or email both reps often. Only pressure works.

Replace the Electoral College

- Determine if your state has joined the states pledging their Electors to the candidate that wins the national popular vote. (www.nationalpopularvote.com)
- If they have not, find out if a bill has been submitted in your legislature and campaign for its passage or ask your representative to introduce it. Tell them you are expecting that one person, one vote is the standard they need to implement.

Campaign Finance Reform

- Support the Fair Elections Now Act, which enhances the power of small donors and offers a public campaign finance system. Follow this link for more information: https://commoncause.org/democracy-wire/fair-elections-now-introduced/

- Urge your Senators and Congressional Representative to take ethical action by introducing a law banning members of Congress from working for a lobbying firm for a term of 5-7 years after they leave office.
- Americans for Campaign Reform at www.idealist.org
- Support constitutional amendment reversing Citizens United https://movetoamend.org
- Find out about your elected representative's fundraising activities at Center for responsive Politics at Open Secrets http://www.opensecrets.org
- Study the public financing laws of Arizona, Connecticut, Maine and the proposal in New York, to determine the best national reform model.
- Buy *Lesterland* – Lessig priced it intentionally at $1.99. Read the book in your book club and host a meeting in your home to discuss putting the People back in power. Invite someone who has differing views than you – remember we all have to do this together.

Inequality and Moral Issues

Rev. Dr. William Barber, former NCAA national board member and now founder of The Poor Peoples campaign is our present day Rev. Dr. Martin Luther King. You can read his most recent book *The Third Reconstruction: How a*

Moral Movement Is Overcoming the Politics of Fear and Division. He has organized moral protests across the nation against undemocratic voter laws, equality in education, protection of Medicare, inequities in legal punishment, worker's rights, living wages and a clear, just immigration system. You can join activities in your area by contacting the Poor People's Campaign: A National Call for Moral Revival at info@poorpeoplescampaign.org

APPENDIX

Greg's Corner
Book Review

The American Dream vs. The Gospel of Wealth: The Fight for a Productive Middle-Class Economy
Norton Garfinkle
Yale University Press
ISBN-13: 978-0-300-10860-6

In many ways, on the surface, it appears that since 2001 we have realized a long-term goal of many economists and politicians alike: an economy with a growing GDP (Gross Domestic Product) relatively low unemployment and an inflationary rate that is in control.

A deeper look at these economic indicators however finds a more disconcerting picture. American workers arc being priced out of owning their own homes. A recent Reuters article cited the nonprofit Center for Housing Policy study. According to the study the median home price is $248,000 requiring an annual income of $85,000.

Additionally, distribution of income figures indicate continuing disparity between the top income levels and all the rest of us. In other words, the middle-class continues to shrink and is indeed under attack. To quote Paul Krugman in his December 14, 2006 Rolling Stone article *The Great Wealth Transfer* "...And while Bush's tax cuts shaved only a few hundred dollars off the tax bills of most Americans, they saved the richest one percent more than an $44,000 on average....But what is happening under Bush is something entirely unprecedented: For the first time in our history, so much growth is being siphoned off to a small, wealthy minority that most Americans are failing to gain ground even during a time of economic growth—and they know it. Today, we're (America) completely out of line with other advanced countries. The share of income received by the top 0.1 percent of Americans is twice the share received by the corresponding group in Britain, and three times the share in France. These days to find societies as unequal as the United States, you have to look beyond the advanced world, to Latin America. And if that comparison doesn't frighten you, it should."

Norton Garfinkle's book does a superb job of providing a very readable survey of American economic history. Our economic history is vital to understand if we wish to place into context what is actually happening in the economic debates of today. Nothing less than the protection of our own economic self-interest and the health of our society is at stake.

The title of the book indicates the two competing economic views that have influenced our society and politicians since the founding of our country. Which set of policies and economic practices benefit America the most?

Do laissez-faire policies promoting the least government intervention as the greatest economic good increase incomes for all? Do lower tax rates for the wealthy generate the greatest economic well being? Are the wealthy the true entrepreneurs that stimulate most of our job growth? (Supply-side economics—The Gospel of Wealth)

Alternatively, do policies which promote and reward hard work and allow as many people as possible to attain a middle-class living really work? These policies also include an active role for government to assist in the expansion of economic opportunities and restrict economic exploitation and injustice. (Demand-side economics – The American Dream)

Garfinkle's book gives Abraham Lincoln the credit he is due for being the first to grasp that the role of government was to clear the path for individuals to achieve as much as possible, and that a slave-based, aristocratic economic system would not allow America to prosper. More than the political differences over states rights, the Civil War was ultimately about the competing economic philosophies and which vision would allow the majority to prosper.

The economic Gospel of Wealth has been presented to us under different guises throughout the years. First was the cold-hearted Social Darwinism of the Gilded Age, which was eventually refuted by William Jennings Bryan, Theodore Roosevelt and Woodrow Wilson. Then came the laissez-faire policies of the 1920s that resulted in the Great Crash and the catastrophic consequences of the Depression including unemployment exceeding 25 percent. In more recent times, Ronald Reagan and George W. Bush's presidencies, we know the Gospel of Wealth as supply-side economics.

By providing extensive research, charts and tables, Garfinkle explodes all of the economic myths of supply-side economics and proves that the policies do not stimulate economic growth. The book also shows the effect of reductions in marginal tax rates, the segments of society the tax cuts have benefited and income distribution figures in America. Most striking of all are the results proving that demand-side economic policies have provided solid results that benefit the majority of Americans. Fiscal policy coupled with sound monetary policies provide us the economic tools to allow all Americans to achieve higher standards of living and the American Dream. We need to deploy these tools for the benefit of the majority not the few.

To quote Garfinkle "The central claim of the supply-side school – that low top marginal income tax rates lead to increased investment, employment, and GDP growth is not supported by the empirical evidence. Given that cuts in the top marginal income tax rate have also increased income equality – and that supply-side tax cuts have resulted in large federal deficits – history's verdict on supply-side tax policy is likely to be unfavorable."

So beware. The next time a politician, any politician, feeds you any of the supply-side rationale, tell them you know the truth. Only when Americans take the time to know the facts can they reject the voodoo economics called supply-side. In reality it is the Gospel of Taking Your Wealth. Let's refute, once and for all, this failed economic argument. I encourage you to read this book.

SOURCES

A More Perfect Union: The Making of the United States Constitution by William Peters, Crown Publishers

Profiles in Courage by John Fitzgerald Kennedy, Harper Collins

Fear by Bob Woodward, Simon and Schuster

On Tryanny: Twenty Lessons from the Twentieth Century by Timothy Snyder, Tim Duggan Books

Is Democracy Dying a series of articles by various authors, Atlantic Magazine, October 2018

The Birth of a New American by Mathhew Stewart, Atlantic Magazine, June 2018

America is not a Democracy by Yascha Mounk, Atlantic Magazine, March 2018

Dear Mr. Madison, You stuck us with Trump by Edwin M. Yoder Jr., News and Observer, April 27, 2018

How Many Cast Ballots Databank AARP Magazine, August 2018

Lesterland: The Corruption of Congress and How to End It by Lawrence Lessig, TED Books

NC's GOP Legislators are back for More Punishing of the Poor by Gene Nichol, News and Observer, May 25,2018

ALEC's Influence over Lawmaking in State Legislatures by Molly Jackman, Brookings Institution, December 6, 2013

List of ALEC members, PRWatch.org, May 16, 2018

Robert F. Kennedy reached across Americas divide by Gene Nichol, News and Observer, June 3, 2018

US debt might soon cost more than the military by Nelson D Schwartz, New York Times, September 30, 2018

America's Debt Dilemma by Andrew Sogel, US News, July 20, 2018

The U.S. Debt and How it Got So Big by Kimberly Amadeo, TheBalance.com, Investopia.com, September 2018

3 charts that show why the US should stop ignoring its debt problem by Elizabeth Schulze, CNBC.com